GUIDE TO LEGAL WRITING STYLE

GUIDE TO LEGAL WRITING STYLE

THIRD EDITION

TERRI LeCLERCQ

*Senior Lecturer and
Fellow, Norman Black Professorship
in Ethical Communication in Law
University of Texas School of Law*

ASPEN
PUBLISHERS

1185 Avenue of the Americas, New York, NY 10036
www.aspenpublishers.com

Permissions
Aspen Publishers
1185 Avenue of the Americas
New York, NY 10036

Printed in the United States of America.

1 2 3 4 5 6 7 8 9 0

ISBN 0-7355-4041-1

Library of Congress Cataloging-in-Publication Data

LeClercq, Terri, 1946-
   Guide to legal writing style / Terri LeClercq — 3rd ed.
     p. cm.
   Includes index.
   ISBN 0-7355-4041-1 (alk. paper)
   1. Legal composition. 2. Law—United States—Language. I. Title.
KF250 .L3913 2004
808'.06634—dc22   2003061211

About Aspen Publishers

Aspen Publishers, headquartered in New York City, is a leading information provider for attorneys, business professionals, and law students. Written by preeminent authorities, our products consist of analytical and practical information covering both U.S. and international topics. We publish in the full range of formats, including updated manuals, books, periodicals, CDs, and online products.

Our proprietary content is complemented by 2,500 legal databases, containing over 11 million documents, available through our Loislaw division. Aspen Publishers also offers a wide range of topical legal and business databases linked to Loislaw's primary material. Our mission is to provide accurate, timely, and authoritative content in easily accessible formats, supported by unmatched customer care.

To order any Aspen Publishers title, go to *www.aspenpublishers.com* or call 1-800-638-8437.

To reinstate your manual update service, call 1-800-638-8437.

For more information on Loislaw products, go to *www.loislaw.com* or call 1-800-364-2512.

For Customer Care issues, e-mail *CustomerCare@aspenpublishers.com;* call 1-800-234-1660; or fax 1-800-901-9075.

Aspen Publishers
A Wolters Kluwer Company

Dedication

Major Donald Lee Miller, 1923-2003

This book was written to help the many legal writing faculty who have such enormous jobs: if law students will work through these pages and apply these style principles to their drafts, then perhaps the faculty will be free to concentrate on analysis; on effective teaching technique; on research; on effective feedback; on student progress; on developing their professional programs; on winning the respect of their faculties, administrators, and students.

I am grateful for the institutional support of University of Texas and the personal support of Jack Getman.

Special thanks to

Editors Betsy Kenney, Ran Satija, Curt Berkowitz,
and Jay Boggis

Students in 2003 Editing for Editors class:

Amy Faulkner	Heidi Frahm
Eliza Hirst	Michael Johnson
Vicki Johnson	Heather Jones
Matt Kacsmaryk	Ashley Kever
Philip Lamb	Mitul Shah
Shannon Snead	Brantley Starr
	Leah Taylor

SUMMARY
OF CONTENTS

CONTENTS

MESSAGE TO STUDENTS

So here you are in law school, and it's back to learning how to write. Why?

WHY STUDY WRITING—AGAIN?

No matter what academic and life experiences you've already had, you will immediately realize that legal writing is yet another skill. And, like any new skill, it has to be practiced.

Yes, it's still writing, but it is a **branch** of technical writing with its own set of rules and priorities. Although you learned to write in grade school, compose essays and organize reports in high school, and perhaps created analytic discussions in college or on the job, there's more! Each of those writing stages helped you reach the next stage—and the next stage. Now you've reached a narrowed branch within the field of technical writing. It's tricky, and it's contradictory. If you can allow yourself some distance from the first writing assignment, though, you'll discover that legal writing reflects the very skill you learn in your law classes: getting to the legal issue and comparing/contrasting that to other cases and policies.

When you begin writing legal documents for class, your first draft will follow the outline your legal faculty provides or your legal-writing text suggests. Formulaic? So was learning to play the piano. Novice musicians have to know the scales before they can leap off into their own creations; so, too, you need to practice the basic outlines for legal writing.

Legal writing is demanding in ways that undergraduate writing rarely is, perhaps because legal writing requires you to be simultaneously precise and concise. Each term in an agreement is chosen for a reason, and yet courts' page limitations can prevent you from including those precise words as you argue about them in your brief. Your signature will signal that you've done the best you can do. If you turn in hastily written documents in law school, you'll probably turn out hastily written documents when you are actually an attorney. That makes sense, doesn't it, because you'll have practiced sliding by instead of performing to the best of your ability.

WHY WASTE TIME ON WRITING SKILLS?
(Or, didn't I come here for torts?)

It's not easy to meet the new demands of law school; new terminology, excessive daily readings, and complicated abstractions create insecurity in even the most confident students. It is natural, then, to focus on learning the information in torts and contracts. That alone takes more time than anyone has, and yet there's a legal-writing skills class, too.

Your writing faculty will offer feedback—to aid students to think and write like the lawyers they will become, organizing and analyzing and applying facts. Unfortunately, many students revert to a defensive posture and insist that they came to law school to study doctrine only—not to review basic writing skills. Thus they try to circumvent the very process that will help them learn doctrine: that of analyzing cases and organizing their thoughts toward a better understanding of the law. Other law students give it the old undergraduate sideswipe and hope it suffices until they have time to really concentrate on writing.

Those reactions are mistakes—costly mistakes.

Practicing legal writing is practicing the law. Learning to be concise is learning to focus on the essential issue and cut extraneous arguments. Learning to find the precise case precedent and precise word is learning to analyze. That's what law school is about, and it's how writing fits into the practice of law.

WHY IS THIS NEW AUDIENCE SO DEMANDING?

(Or, if I sound smart enough, won't I be able to get by?)

Visualize an audience of hurried, irritated, and probably bored readers (does this describe your first-year study group as well?). You must convince them that you have something they need to read and that your position is correct. Your memorandum or brief or letter is not the most important part of your readers' day; it's only part of their job:

- They are not reading it uninterrupted.
- They are not reading it during mental prime time.
- They are not interested in the law for law's sake.
- They do not expect to be entertained or amused.
- They do not want to focus on your writing style.

Somehow, you have to get them to read what you've written, and to act on your ideas or conclusions. That's your job.

In undergraduate school, it was the professor's job to read student writing. A student's job was just to turn in his or her best work (although most of us can remember turning in a "draft" as a final paper—and getting away with it). When graduates leave and start their professional roles, though, they have to fulfill the professional expectations of their audiences—just as soon as they guess who the audience is and what that new audience expects.

IF LEGAL WRITING IS SO IMPORTANT, WHY ARE MY TEXTBOOKS FULL OF CONVOLUTED OPINIONS?

(Or, is someone kidding?)

Not many readers can defend the prose of judicial opinions selected for case books—a style students instinctively assume is "the way law looks." We can't defend this prose because it is so very terrible—you're right. Perhaps you can get some perspective if you realize that

- the case may have been written **years ago** when writers used a more lofty, elevated language,

- casebook authors cut and paste pieces of cases chosen **not** for their prose style but **for the issues** they present, and
- there are a lot of bad writers in the legal profession—but **don't join** them!

Historically, legal prose was both dense and confusing. Critics of that prose theorize that early writers needed both Latin and French terminology to meet the needs of a linguistically varied audience, and that the audience expected an elevated style to reflect the somber nature of the law. Some even more cynical critics insist that early legal writers wanted to make the law unobtainable to the layman so that society would always need attorneys.

Few readers today expect Latin and French equivalents, and most are depressed rather than impressed when they see a page of legal prose. Remember your frustration when you read your casebooks—you don't want your readers to respond that way to your own prose.

HOW CAN I MAKE BEST USE OF THIS BOOK?

1. Skim this book before beginning your first assignment; you'll see what is important to your new field.

2. After completing your first draft, check your organization against the suggestions in Chapter 1. Evaluate your sentences using the guide of Chapter 2. Make sure you haven't misused any new or unusual words by comparing yours to those in Chapter 3. Double-check the rules of punctuation set out in Chapter 4 to ensure that you use the conventions of legal punctuation. Finally, compare your visual format to the readable examples in Chapter 5, and then you're ready to turn in your final version to the professor.

3. When your paper is returned, focus on the professor's feedback and return to any chapter that offers advice in those areas. If your professor had trouble following your analysis, perhaps you need to revise the road map or topic sentences. Carefully reread the advice of Chapter 1. Similarly, if your reader asked questions about your sentence style or word choice, review Chapters 2 and 3. You

may learn that your punctuation (or lack of) created substantive questions; if so, return to Chapter 4 for help. Practice the exercises in the Appendix and the CD.

With this focus on improvement, you won't make the same mistakes again. You'll grow as a legal writer. Then, after repeated practice throughout law school, you can enter the legal profession unworried about an opposing counsel who is paid just to scrutinize your document for weakness in your analysis or ambiguities in your prose.

This book cannot answer all of your style questions or calm all of your anxieties. But if you use it as a springboard for constant and deliberate practice, you'll develop into a careful legal writer.

January 2004   *Terri LeClercq*

GUIDE
TO LEGAL
WRITING
STYLE

✦ ✦ ✦

Only as we tumble our words onto the page or into a dictating machine do we begin to see our story, our argument, take shape. The time to focus on the relationships between the disparate parts of our document is during the reading of the first draft. Only then can we see that point one is independent of point two, but that points three and four are inexorably tied to the outcome of point two and thus dependent.

TERRI LECLERQ, *EXPERT LEGAL WRITING* 60 (1995)

✦ ✦ ✦

1

ORGANIZING WITH STYLE

After thinking about the facts of a case and tentatively identifying the problem, writers generally produce a hash of ideas, marginalia, and cases. **It's a draft.**

Now, how do we get from a draft to a final product that must lead readers through the writer's ideas and the legal precedent behind those ideas? Some writers, naturally organized, begin with an outline that they fill in as the research develops. Others flail about, scribbling and drawing arrows until they understand what it is they're writing about. Whatever a writer's preliminary organizational strategy, readers will have to follow the resulting progression of ideas. That's why as a writer, you need to reserve time beyond what's required for the initial researching and scribbling. Legal writers must tackle the draft again, with a fresh eye, to decide how best to help readers find what they need. Deciding on your macro and micro organization should be your first step.

Macro (overall) organization includes a general introduction, an indication of the order and cohesion of major points, and your conclusion. Micro (paragraph) level is your paragraph development and internal cohesion. If you give readers a strong introduction and follow it logically, readers can skim the introduction and headings, and quickly learn both what the document is about and how the parts fit together.

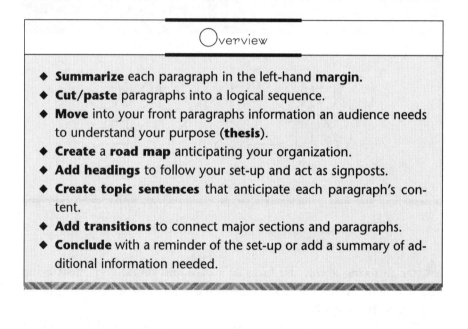

Overview

- **Summarize** each paragraph in the left-hand **margin.**
- **Cut/paste** paragraphs into a logical sequence.
- **Move** into your front paragraphs information an audience needs to understand your purpose (**thesis**).
- **Create** a **road map** anticipating your organization.
- **Add headings** to follow your set-up and act as signposts.
- **Create topic sentences** that anticipate each paragraph's content.
- **Add transitions** to connect major sections and paragraphs.
- **Conclude** with a reminder of the set-up or add a summary of additional information needed.

ORGANIZING YOUR RESEARCH: MARGIN OUTLINES

A useful technique for evaluating what you've uncovered through research and drafting is to type out your ideas as you've scribbled them, putting them into whatever order seems best for the moment. That can mean typing case summaries first, or your list of policy considerations, etc. Just get them down. (Don't throw away your notes, because you'll undoubtedly need them later.) Print them out and see what you've got.

In the margin of that draft copy, jot one word or phrase that summarizes each paragraph's main point. Then quickly read through your marginalia, checking to see if they follow a logical order. If they do, decide whether that order fulfills your audience's needs. If not, you can rearrange with a massive cut-and-paste. Sometimes you'll be able to delete whole paragraphs of repeated material.

A major obstacle that novice legal writers must overcome is the temptation to organize case by case. You need to practice legal thought, and thus writing, as a progression of issues (not cases). Then you support those issues with authority, the cases.

INTRODUCTION: THESIS AND ROAD MAP

After moving your draft sections into a logical order, you need to create an introduction (which may be the first paragraph, or several) that includes:

- a **thesis** announcing your major point or conclusion and
- a **road map** announcing your organization.

This internal cueing anticipates the major point(s) and divisions of your argument, which allows readers to feel comfortable with what follows. A comfortable reader is a grateful reader.

The introductory paragraphs explain your main **thesis** (usually your conclusion) in the context of the overall issue. Some legal readers expect to find the conclusion attached to specific facts; others don't. If the overall thesis depends on several legal points, you should begin each section with a small-scale version of the introductory thesis and road map.

In addition to the thesis, you will create a **road map**, which is a textual outline of the information to follow. The road map lets readers know in advance the relative *weight* of the parts and the *order* in which they will be discussed.

Thesis statements vary by function: the thesis of a *memorandum*, for example, is predictive, leading the reader from the legal issue to a short, general conclusion that is afterwards supported by a balanced,

3

analytic survey of pertinent theories and cases. In contrast, the thesis of a *brief* is persuasive rather than predictive, and thus announces a conclusion supported through cases and policy.

A **road map** foreshadows the organizational pattern to follow. It might, for instance, be a quick overview of three exceptions to a general rule. Or it might be a list of theories that you will examine. Like a literal road map, it lets travelers (your readers) know how long they will be on the road, what they will find the most interesting, and which minor roads to expect along the way.

Look at the following examples from different legal documents and examine the introduction, the set-up, and the road maps for these different formats and audiences.

A brief:

thesis ▶ | The defendant should be liable for malpractice because he was negligent in failing to properly research settled law. Historically, the law has placed a duty on lawyers to research properly. <u>Morrill v. Grimes</u>, 27 Tex. 646, 651 (1864). This court has recently updated that duty to say that failure to meet this standard by failing to properly analyze precedent is a breach. <u>Two Thirty None Joint Venture v. Joe</u>, 60 S.W.3d 896, 905 (Tex. App. Dallas 2001—pet. granted). The lawyer will not be liable, however, if the law in the area is unsettled. Because the court issued a decision in this area, because a reasonably prudent lawyer would have easily found the decision, and because this failure caused the plaintiff harm, the defendant should be liable for malpractice.

A road ▶ map predicts organization

repeated ▶ thesis

A law journal article:

The Security Housing Unit at Pelican Bay State Prison near Crescent City, California, is the last stop in California's penal system. It was in this unit that Vaughn Dortcha, a prisoner with a life-long history of mental

4

introduction ▶ problems, was confined after a conviction for grand theft. There, the stark conditions of isolation caused his mental condition to deteriorate, to the point that he "smeared himself repeatedly with feces and urine." . . . Ultimately, six guards wearing rubber gloves held Vaughn, with his hands cuffed behind his back, in a tub of scalding water. . . . After about fifteen minutes, when Vaughn was finally allowed to stand, his skin peeled off in sheets, "hanging in large clumps around his legs." . . . He went into shock and almost died. . . . Pelican Bay Warden Charles Marshall attributed the incident to an "inexperienced staff" and "the difficulties of opening a new prison."

thesis ▶ This Comment argues that, rather than being a model for the rest of the nation . . . Pelican Bay State prison inflicts unacceptable psychological trauma on inmates confined in the virtually unrelieved isolation of the Security Housing and Violence Control Units . . . [and] as a result of this isolation violates the Eighth Amendment of the United States Constitution in that it constitutes cruel and unusual punishment.

roadmap ▶
paragraph Part II provides a brief history of the American penitentiary . . . Part III describes the physical aspects of Pelican Bay and the general conditions of confinement within the Security Housing Unit (SHU) and the Violence Control Unit (VCU). Part IV demonstrates that the particular effects of sensory deprivation . . . violate the Eighth Amendment. . . . The Comment concludes with a summary of the argument and a discussion of the negative societal effects that result when psychologically damaged SHU inmates are released directly into our cities and towns.

Source: Sally Mann Romano, *If the SHU Fits: Cruel and Unusual Punishment at California's Pelican Bay State Prison*, 45 EMORY L. J. 1089–1092 (1996).

USING HEADINGS AS SIGNPOSTS

Long documents *require* headings; shorter documents are *aided* by them. In either case, your readers will benefit from the quick overview of the larger picture in your thesis and set-up, and can then skim your headings. As a writer, you will also benefit when you take time to summarize the paragraphs' contents as headings: if the headings you add to the first draft don't summarize your discussion when you skim them, or if the headings bounce you around from one idea to another, you are now on alert to make the necessary adjustments to your draft.

Guidelines for Headings

A bonus for careful writers is the visual effect of headings: readers can be pulled by the headings and subheadings to the section of specific interest.

1. Headings need to **satisfy the readers' needs**. Headings labeled "Element One," "Element Two," and "Element Three" do not satisfy anything. Instead, a heading should summarize the material within that block of text.

2. Headings should **reflect the set-up.** If you insert a major heading to introduce one element of negligence but do not use headings for the following two, your reader won't understand that those three elements are parallel.

3. Headings can consist of single words, phrases, or sentences, but they should **be consistent in content and grammatical structure.** If the first major heading is a full sentence, then all the other major headings should be full sentences. Similarly, the subheadings may be only phrases, but then each subheading should be a phrase.

4. Headings should be **consistent in typography**; if major subheadings are flush left and in bold face, then sub-subheadings need to be differentiated as a group by a consistent indent, or they should be in italics. Some courts have specific guidelines for headings in certain filings, but others do not, so you should investigate before assuming that one format will work for any document.

5. Headings should be **independent of the text** that follows them. The following portion of a brief relies on its heading for its logic; if readers skipped the heading, they would find themselves in the middle of a fact discussion that has no legal context. The writer has left the context back up in the heading and has forgotten to reestablish it within the textual discussion.

> **X** *Hunter* Raises Serious Issues Surrounding the Timeliness of a Rule 11 Motion.

The district court's Show Cause Order was issued April 1998. However, the Sanctions Order was not issued until October 2000, a delay of two and a half years. While sanctions may be imposed when a case is no longer pending, the inordinate delay here contravened the rule's purpose.

Try These

First, skim only the introductory paragraph. Next, evaluate the headings that follow. Are these headings a reasonable follow-up to the introductory paragraph? See answers, page 103.

1. If the measure for malpractice is the "reasonably competent practitioner standard," clients will not be able to overcome the great burden of proving that their attorneys acted unreasonably. Frank Cosgrove sustained injuries as the result of an automobile accident. After the expiration of the limitations period, Mr. Cosgrove discovered that his attorney, Walter Grimes, had filed suit against the wrong person and alleged the wrong location. Mr. Cosgrove wants to file a malpractice action against his attorney alleging neg-

ligence, breach of contract, false representations, and Deceptive Trades Practices Act violations. The court will probably hold that the first two charges fall within the "reasonably competent" standard, but will reject the DTPA charge.

a. The court investigated the "subjective good faith" excuse and found that there is no excuse for attorney negligence.

b. His attorney had stated that he had indeed filed the lawsuit, when in fact he had left the task to another attorney and failed to ensure the filing.

c. The court would not award mental anguish damages for the false representation or DTPA claims.

2. **Next, read the paragraph below and create your own headings that would logically follow this introductory paragraph.**

An appellate lawyer must consistently serve his/her client by mastering the record, thoroughly researching the law, and exercising judgment in identifying arguments that may be advanced on appeal. Yolanda Denise Walder used court-appointed counsel to file a brief in which her counsel argued that the State failed to prove that Walder's failure to pay her (earlier) fine and community service was intentional, and that the trial court denied her right to counsel by denying her a continuance. The brief cited one case, one statute, and one constitutional provision as support. The appellate court determined Walder's brief was deficient because it did not provide adequate citations to pertinent legal authority. The Sixth Amendment requires appellate counsel to render effective assistance on behalf of his clients. Case law has interpreted the amendment to cover thorough research of the law. Quite simply, the Rule of Appellate Procedure 38.1 provides clear guidelines for the form of a brief.

a. _____

b. _____

c. _____

3. **Evaluate this heading and its supporting first paragraph.**

c. The Oregon Supreme Court, in the recent *In re Gatti*, 8 P.3d 966 (Or. 2000), sanctioned a lawyer who misrepresented his identity while attempting to investigate a claim of insurance fraud.

Thus, the Oregon court refused to recognize "an exception for any lawyer to engage in dishonesty." *In re Gatti* at 976. Not all states adopt as strict an approach. New York, for example, has long recognized prosecutorial exceptions to the dishonesty rule.

USEFULNESS OF TOPIC SENTENCES

Topic sentences work in much the same way as a thesis (see pages 3-4): they introduce the idea within the paragraph; they set boundaries for the paragraph; and they help tie ideas together. Perhaps some paragraphs won't require a specific topic sentence—still, they'll need cueing transitions to help readers stay on track.

Quickly skim the following student memorandum looking **only** at each paragraph's topic sentence.

MEMORANDUM

Subject: Lima's legal malpractice claim against Gerardi for failure to Shepardize

QUESTION PRESENTED: Does an attorney commit malpractice when he cites a case that has been overturned and this results in an adverse decision in litigation?

CONCLUSION: Yes. An attorney who cites to an overturned case does not act as a reasonably prudent attorney. If the failure results in harm to the client, the attorney is negligent and thus has committed malpractice.

9

FACTS: Our client, Lima, Inc., an importer of limes, was represented by John Gerardi in a litigation matter. In his brief, Gerardi relied heavily on a case that, unknown to him, the Texas Supreme Court had overturned six months before Lima's scheduled hearing. Lima lost the case and was forced to pay $250,000 in damages. The court explicitly made its decision based on Gerardi's reliance on the overturned decision and admonished Gerardi for his failure to Shepardize. Lima has engaged us to sue Gerardi for malpractice.

▶ DISCUSSION: Lima's malpractice claim against Gerardi hinges on the legal issue of negligence, particularly the extent of Gerardi's duty to research the law properly and the breach of this duty. In Texas, a malpractice claim is based on the law of negligence. Cosgrove v. Grimes, 774 S.W.2d 662, 664 (Tex. 1989). To show that Gerardi was negligent, Lima must show that Gerardi had a duty to Lima, that he breached it, and that this breach was the proximate cause of Lima's harm. Cosgrove, 774 S.W.2d at 665. An attorney has a duty to properly research the law, and breaches this duty when he fails to do so. Morrill v. Graham, 27 Tex. 646, 651 (1864); Walder v. Texas, 85 S.W.3d 824, 827 (Ct. App.—Waco 2002). Failure to check legal precedents is a breach of this duty. Two Thirty Nine Joint Venture v. Joe, 60 S.W.3d 896, 905 (Tex. App. Dallas 2001—pet. granted); Texas Disciplinary R. Prof'l Conduct, 1.01. Cmt. 3 (2002). Where the breach proximately causes harm to the client, the attorney will be liable for malpractice. Two Thirty Nine Joint Venture, 60 S.W.3d at 896.

▶ An attorney has a duty to research the law properly and breaches this duty when he fails to do so. When a lawyer undertakes a matter on behalf of a client, the lawyer must exercise ordinary care and diligence in handling the client's matter, including using the skills normally possessed by competent lawyers. Savings Bank v. Ward, 100 U.S. 195, 199 (1879). The lawyer breaches his duty to his client when he fails to meet this standard. Savings Bank, 100 U.S.

at 199. The duty to properly perform legal research is a universally recognized attribute of the competent lawyer. For example, the rules of professional responsibility in Texas comment that attorney competence requires "thoroughness in the study and analysis of the law and facts." Texas Disciplinary R. Prof'l Conduct, 1.01, Cmt. 1 (2002). Numerous cases in Texas and other jurisdictions have echoed this position. *See, e.g.*, Morrill v. Graham, 27 Tex. 646, 651 (1864); Walder, 85 S.W.3d at 827; Smith v. Lewis, 530 P.2d 589, 595 (Cal. 1975). The court in Walder, quoting the U.S. Supreme Court, stated that "every advocate has essentially the same professional responsibility . . . [to] thoroughly research the law." Walder, 85 S.W.3d at 827, *quoting* McCoy v. Court of Appeals, 486 U.S. 429, 438 (1988).

▶ Checking cases to see whether they are still reliable precedent is a central part of a lawyer's responsibility. The Texas rules of professional responsibility require a lawyer to be able to undertake "the analysis of precedent" to be considered competent. Texas Disciplinary R. Prof'l Conduct, 1.01, Cmt. 3 (2002). Though violation of the rules is not itself considered malpractice, the rules are the basic standard by which to evaluate a lawyer's performance. Two Thirty Nine Joint Venture, 60 S.W.3d at 905. A number of cases have commented on the importance of checking precedents. In Walder, for example, the court lays out, step-by-step, the requirements for proper legal research, including that "counsel should research the subsequent history of any case cited to be sure that it has not been reversed or modified." Walder, 85 S.W.3d at 828.

▶ Gerardi may argue that because the case he relied on was only recently overturned, the law in that area is unsettled, so failure to account for it is not a breach. Where a particular area of law is unsettled, an attorney will not be held liable for failing to know it. Morrill, 27 Tex. at 652. In Morrill, an attorney failed to present a claim against a decedent's estate within the proper time period. The Texas Supreme Court ruled that the attorney was not negligent in failing to do so because the question of whether the presentment was required was an "open and controverted point." Morrill, 27 Tex. at 652. Gerardi would not succeed in his argument, however, because the court further stated that law is settled once it has been "settled by the adjudications of our courts." Morrill, 27 Tex. at 652. Thus, if there has been a decision in an area, the law is no longer considered unsettled. Gerardi may argue that because the decision he failed to discover was relatively recent, he should not be re-quired to find it. The court in Morrill mentions as one factor in de-termining attorney liability, the "difficulty, nay, often the absolute impossibility of access by attorneys to the ordinary sources of in-formation" that prevailed at that time. Morrill, 27 Tex. at 652. However, given advances in communication technology and the proliferation of law libraries since that case was decided, the court will more likely find that a 6-month-old case is well within an at-torney's duty. Lawrence Duncan MacLachlan, Gandy Dancers On The Web: How The Internet Has Raised The Bar On Lawyers' Professional Responsibility To Research And Know The Law, 13 Geo. J. Legal Ethics 607 (2000).

▶ Where the attorney's breach of duty proximately causes harm to his client, the attorney will be liable for malpractice. Two Thirty Nine Joint Venture, 60 S.W.3d at 909. To show causation, we must show that Lima would have won the case but for Gerardi's breach of duty and that this was foreseeable, i.e., that Gerardi should have antici-pated that his failure to research properly would cause injury to his client. Two Thirty Nine Joint Venture, 60 S.W.3d at 909. Normally, the "but-for" is the most difficult part of the negligence action and requires expert testimony, but where the negligence would be ob-vious to a layman, expert testimony is not required. Mazuca v. Schumann, 82 S.W.3d 90, 97 (Ct. App.—San Antonio, 2002, pet. denied). In Mazuca, the attorney wrote a letter to the client stating his responsibility in not filing the client's case properly, and the court ruled that this was strong evidence of obvious malpractice. Mazuca, 82 S.W.3d at 97. Our case is analogous because the court cited Gerardi's failure to Shepardize as the sole reason the case was lost. Because Gerardi is the cause of Lima's damages, he will be liable for the harm caused. The loss of the case forced Lima to pay $250,000 in damages. Harm resulting from malpractice may include financial losses caused by the breach of duty, including the amount necessary to restore the wronged party to its prior position. Two Thirty Nine Joint Venture, 60 S.W.3d at 909.

▶ Because Gerardi had a duty and breached it, and because that breach was the proximate cause of injury, all of the elements of negligence are present. Thus, Lima may sustain a malpractice action against Gerardi.

You were probably able to understand the overall legal question and its substantive support—through those topic sentences alone. Read together, the topic sentences form an elliptical but coherent paragraph.

Topic Sentence 1 explains that the memo is about malpractice, and it narrows malpractice to breach of a specific duty.

Topic Sentence 2 defines the duty.

Topic Sentence 3 narrows the duty to researching reliable precedent.

Topic Sentence 4 provides counteranalysis, so that we learn the other possible interpretation of cases and facts.

Topic Sentence 5 connects malpractice to harm suffered by client.

Topic Sentence 6 analogizes the facts of this case to the facts of Mazuca and concludes that Gerardi will be held liable.

Experiment with your own rough drafts by separating each topic sentence from your text: is each one a strong introduction to, or conclusion about, that paragraph's main idea? Next, examine the coherence of the topic sentences as they relate to the overall set-up. At this point, you may decide that some added transitions will smooth the reader's path.

TRANSITIONS

Transitions may look insignificant, but they perform a critical function in connecting ideas. Whether connecting large-scale segments, paragraphs, sentences, or words, transitions signal relationships.

1. Traditional transitions explain those relationships right up front: *again, once, first, finally, however.* As the writer, it is your job to connect words and ideas so that your readers don't have to do the mental work for you. Your legal readers should be able to trace how you structure your discussions, descriptions, and arguments by focusing on these transitions. A carefully placed "on the other hand" immediately alerts your reader, just as "in a similar case" does.

2. Repetition of words/ideas can create cohesion, as can **dovetailing** (using words with a similar linguistic base like "deny" and "denial"[1]).

> Gerardi will have **two arguments. First**, he will **argue** that the case he relied on was only recently overturned, and thus the law in that area could be considered **unsettled**. Where a particular area of law is **unsettled**, an attorney will not be held liable for failing to know it. **Morrill v. Graham**, 27 Tex. 646, 652 (1864). **In Morrill**, an attorney failed to **present** a claim against a decedent's estate within the proper time period. Whether the **presentment** was required, the Texas Supreme Court ruled, was an "open and contoverted point, **so** the attorney was not negligent in failing to present the claim." Morrill, 27 Tex. at 652. **This first argument** cannot be successful, **though**, because the court further stated that law is **settled** once it has been "**settled by the adjudications** of our courts." Morrill, 27 Tex. at 652. The legal

---

[1] See, for instance, the detailed discussions of dovetailing in Laurel Oates, Anne Enquist, and Kelly Kunsch, The Legal Writing Handbook 159-60, 621-31, 3d. ed. Aspen (2002).

issue was **adjudicated** when the Texas Supreme Court issued a decision on the point, thus **settling** the law according to the Morrill court's definition.

Second, Gerardi may argue that because the decision he failed to discover was relatively recent, he should **therefore** not be required to find it. He is correct that Morrill mentions, as one factor in determining attorney liability, the "difficulty, nay, often the absolute **impossibility of access** by attorneys to the ordinary sources of information" that prevailed at that time. Morrill, 27 Tex. at 652. Morrill was decided in **1864**. **From 1864 to 2003, however**, communication technology and the proliferation of law libraries have significantly improved the **possibilities of access** to ordinary sources of information by any attorney. **Therefore**, in response to Gerardi's **second argument**, the court will more likely find that knowledge of a 6-month-old case is well within an attorney's duty.

3. Case names and citation information rarely function as effective topic sentences. When readers begin a paragraph without an effective topic sentence, they cannot assimilate a new case name and citation into the textual flow.

There is no right or wrong way to organize; effective organization is determined by both the audience and the message. Focusing specifically on organization, however, will help to review your thought process and logic as you develop thesis, road map, headings, topic sentences, and transitions.

Examining Your Micro Organization

Here's a useful tip for examining the organization of your draft: cut the draft into paragraph blocks, scramble the blocks, and reassemble them to their original order using only the topic sentences and transitions. If you must reread each of your own paragraphs to recognize their content, imagine how difficult it would be for your reader to follow what you are saying! Better return to the draft and sharpen your internal cues.

If you want to tighten your document even more, cut one of your paragraphs into separate sentences, mix up its sentences, and ask a friend to reorganize the paragraph. If your friend can't find the topic sentence and reassemble the original, return to that draft. You're not finished.

After reviewing the following paragraphs, delete unnecessary detail, reorder the sentences, and add transitions so that the paragraphs have coherence and focus on the legal competency of lawyers and summer clerks. See answer, page 104.

Annette Noel occupied the last office in the summer associate hallway. None of the offices had a window. Hers had a fold-down desk top that retracted so that librarians could reach file cabinets along the back wall. Ms Noel had taken first-year Legal Research and Writing among the five courses she was required to take last year. She understood that federal and state laws were both dependent and independent. Jones and Jones, Inc. (J & J) hired 35 summer associates for its Dallas office. J & J's goal was to find 12–15 promising students who would work for J & J after graduation. Ms Noel's undergraduate background was in business, because her family imported pottery.

On Friday afternoon, July 5, Ms Noel was in her office when Gerald Gerardi walked the hall looking for research help. He pulled a chair into her doorway, sat, and told her he needed a memo on Texas regulations for food safety and pesticides by Monday at 9 a.m. Questions? Ms Noel didn't know what to ask. Over the weekend, Ms Noel researched and wrote a 40-page memorandum. No law librarians worked that weekend. On

Monday, Gerardi used her memo to file his brief for his biggest client, Lima, Inc. On July 12, Ms Noel left for her second summer internship in New York City.

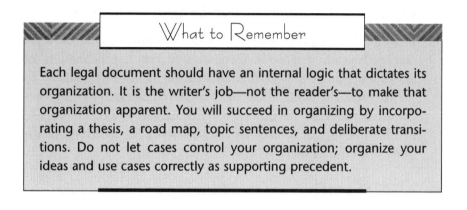

What to Remember

Each legal document should have an internal logic that dictates its organization. It is the writer's job—not the reader's—to make that organization apparent. You will succeed in organizing by incorporating a thesis, a road map, topic sentences, and deliberate transitions. Do not let cases control your organization; organize your ideas and use cases correctly as supporting precedent.

CONCLUDING EXERCISES

See answers, page 105.

1. **Thesis and road maps.** Many readers would not be able to follow the road map paragraph below. What is the problem, and how would you correct it?

Rule 11 of the Federal Rules of Civil Procedure requires attorneys to certify that any pleading or written motion is filed not to harass, or to delay, and to certify that the claims and contentions are not frivolous. In the instant case, Powe believed that his motion on behalf of the teacher was backed by strong evidence that she had been discriminated against by her administration. He had no knowledge of a Fourth Circuit requirement that a client must go through collective bargaining as a member of a school district. Thus, he counseled her not to ask for collective bargaining before the filing.

   a. Powe should not be sanctioned because he had evidence of discrimination.

b. The administration withheld documents that were needed for a timely review.

2. **Road map paragraphs and headings.** Are the headings following the paragraph below anticipated? Are they effective?

Powe's evidence probably proves that his motion on behalf of the teacher was not frivolous. Generally, federal courts are lenient about accepting evidence that an attorney is not filing merely to waste time. The Fourth Circuit, however, has established precedent that collective bargaining is required before a complaint can be filed in court. Several other circuits have discussed but not applied this requirement.

a. The General Rule and the Fourth Circuit's Requirement

b. Case Law

c. Counter analysis

3. **Topic sentences and transitions.** Rewrite the following draft paragraph so that readers can anticipate its contents and follow its reasoning.

In <u>Walder</u>, the court ruled that a counsel must serve a client to the best of his or her ability. <u>Walder v. Texas</u>, 85 S.W.3d 824, 829 (2002). There, counsel did not identify the appropriate standard for appellate review of a revocation order. In <u>Cosgrove</u>, the Texas Supreme Court ruled that counsel had a duty to act as a reasonably prudent professional. There, counsel did not recognize the statute of limitations in a car accident that occurred in another state. <u>Cosgrove v. Grimes</u>, 774 S.W.2d 662 (1989). The holdings of these cases were similar. Both courts held that attorneys have a duty of reasonable care to serve their clients. In Mr. Gerardi's case, the issue presented is whether overlooking a major development in case law is reasonable.

4. **Transitions.** Review this memorandum's statement of facts. Reorder sentences, delete unnecessary detail, and add or change transitions to create coherence.

Pamela Hunter filed suit on behalf of a group of bakery workers. She filed a class-action suit in North Carolina. The workers believed that their bakery had violated Title V11 of the Civil Rights Act of 1964 when the bakery closed. Ms Hunter argued that the bakery had a pattern and practice of racial discrimination. Compared to the predominately white workers at other company-owned bakeries, the predominately African-American workers in this bakery were more skilled but paid less. The owners had publicly stated that this store would remain open throughout the year.

The bakery denied the allegations. The bakery insisted that any Title V11 claims had to be arbitrated under a collective bargaining agreement (CBA). The bakery asked the court to impose a Rule 11 sanction on Hunter for filing a lawsuit when she knew or should have known of the CBA. The North Carolina court sanctioned her and suspended her legal practice for five years.

Five other circuits have held that Title V11 claims do not have to be first arbitrated under a CBA.

Take the sentence, "The sky is blue." No junior associate would be so naive as to think this proposition could pass muster in a big firm. . . . [H]e knows enough to say, "The sky is generally blue." [Or, f]or extra syllables, "The sky generally appears to be blue." A senior associate seeing this sentence [making corrections would say:] "In some parts of the world, what is generally thought of as the sky sometimes appears to be blue."

DAN WHITE, THE OFFICIAL LAWYER'S HANDBOOK 177 (1983)

✦ ✦ ✦ ✦

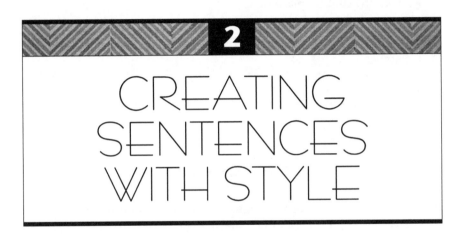

2

CREATING SENTENCES WITH STYLE

It's back to your original draft for a look at readability: Will your readers understand everything on a first read-through, or are your sentences so long and convoluted that your readers will be forced either to reread or to abandon the project?

Predictably, it takes most new law students about a week before they begin producing sentences that resemble those in case books. Giving in to this subliminal seduction is natural, but it is also counterproductive for novices trying to grapple with new legal concepts.

This chapter examines problems that commonly affect the readability of sentence-level legal prose. The idea here is that you'll return to your now-organized draft and tackle each sentence until it specifically says what you want it to say. That requires time—the same sort of time your future legal documents will demand.

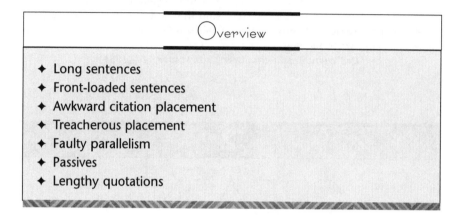

Overview

+ Long sentences
+ Front-loaded sentences
+ Awkward citation placement
+ Treacherous placement
+ Faulty parallelism
+ Passives
+ Lengthy quotations

LONG SENTENCES

Most legal sentences are too long. Open any casebook to a random page and you will find copious examples. Those long sentences are the result of legal training, which, as you are learning, is a process of qualifying, narrowing, and delineating with evidence. Thus, your new skill at qualifying and delineating can force your essential information into a chain of clauses that become long, convoluted sentences.

Not all long sentences are difficult reading, of course; no set number of words or typed lines breaks readability rules.[1] If legal sentences are carefully punctuated and cued, then all those necessary qualifications will not affect the document's readability. Without proper cueing, though, a chain of embedded, dependent clauses will confuse readers:

---

[1] For instance: A mouse is what is eaten or caught by a trap or a rat. Sounds logical? But how can a trap eat a mouse? For a full discussion of this, and other, drafting problems, see DAVID MELLINKOFF, THE LANGUAGE OF THE UNIFORM COMMERCIAL CODE, 77 YALE L. REV. 185, 215 (1967).

introductory citation hides main ▶ subject (Oregon appellate court)	In <u>Portland General Electric Co. v.</u> <u>Duncan, Weinberg, Miller & Pembroke,</u>
judgment (sentence's object) ▶ that allowed=embedded clause	986 P.2d 35 (Or. App. 1999), the appellate court affirmed in part a judgment that al- lowed a firm's Washington, D.C. office to
that the office could not ▶ handle=embedded clause	handle a matter that the firm's Portland office could not handle because of a con-
provided an adequate ▶ screen=dependent clause	flict, provided an adequate screen was set up between the two offices, the appellate
appellate court agreeing= ▶ unnecessary dependent clause	court agreeing that the screen should be approved either by the lower court or by
that the screen ▶ should=embedded clause	the ethics experts who testified in the mat- ter, because the parties in this case had
because the parties=unnecessary ▶ dependent clause	previously consented to a screen on re- lated matters and had a history of mutual trust.

Solutions

1. Where possible, **break** embedded clauses into separate sentences.

Broken into Two Sentences
The appellate court affirmed in part a judgment that allowed a
firm's Washington, D.C. office to handle a matter that the firm's
Portland office could not handle because of a conflict. **The court
required** that the firm provide an adequate screen between the
two offices.

Broken into Two Sentences Plus an Added Transition
The appellate court affirmed in part a judgment that allowed a
firm's Washington, D.C. office to handle a matter that the firm's
Portland office could not handle because of a conflict.
Specifically, the court required that the firm provide an adequate
screen between the two offices.

2. Place the **subject close to the verb** and place both of them toward the beginning of the sentence.

> **X** The appellate **court**, allowing a firm's Washington, D.C. office to handle a matter that the firm's Portland office could not handle because of a conflict, nevertheless **required** an adequate screen set up between the two offices.

The appellate **court required** an adequate screen to be set up between two offices when it allowed a firm's Washington, D.C. office to handle a matter that the firm's Portland office could not handle because of a conflict.

3. **Avoid** excessive coordination and subordination.

The appellate court affirmed in part a judgment that allowed a firm's Washington, D.C. office to handle a matter that the firm's Portland office could not handle because of a conflict. **The court required** that an adequate screen was set up between the two offices. The **court also required** that the screen should be approved either by the lower court or by the ethics experts who testified in the matter. **The court confirmed the judgment because** the parties in this case had previously consented to a screen on related matters and had a history of mutual trust.

4. **Add signposts** if the sentence length is absolutely necessary:

  a. **Add** transitions and dovetail.
  b. **Punctuate** to allow for closure.
  c. **Tabulate** parallel lists and ideas.

TRANSITIONS AND DOVETAIL. Careful **signposting** can help defeat necessarily long sentences by signaling relationships: transitions, repetitions of words or phrases, introductions, and conclusions. (See Chapter 1, Transitions.)

PUNCTUATION SIGNPOSTS. In addition to words used as signposts, **punctuation signposts** can make the message more accessible, as the following colon illustrates:

The court allowed either the lower court or ethics experts to approve the conflict screen for two reasons: the parties had previously consented to a screen, and they had a history of mutual trust.

NUMBERED LISTS (TABULATION). Finally, you can also use **numbered lists (tabulation)** to create an organizational hierarchy (and add white space to the page). The following example, from an attorney's client letter, suffers from both length and embedded clauses, but we can revise it by adding tabulation.

> **X**   When respondents are questioned by suspicious interviewers, subjects tend to view their responses as deceptive even when they are honest, which significantly increases errors in detection of honesty. Two distinct phenomena contribute to these errors: the suspicious interrogation distorts observers' perceptions, and the interrogation causes stress for the respondent, which in turn induces behavior likely to be interpreted as deceptive. This latter phenomenon has been called the "Othello's error," since Othello mistook Desdemona's distress and despair in response to his accusation of infidelity.

Revision

When respondents are questioned by suspicious interviewers, subjects tend to view their responses as deceptive even when they are honest, which significantly increases errors in detection of honesty. Two distinct phenomena contribute to these errors:

1. the suspicious interrogation distorts observers' perceptions, and
2. the interrogation causes stress for the respondent, which in turn induces behavior likely to be interpreted as deceptive.

This latter phenomenon has been called the "Othello's error," since Othello mistook Desdemona's distress and despair in response to his accusation of infidelity.

Thus, as you sharpen your draft, you can use transitions and dovetailing, punctuation, and tabulation to help your readers understand necessarily long sentences.

Try These

Either (1) justify leaving the following sentences at their current length or (2) create a more understandable sentence: break into separate sentences; punctuate or dovetail them for clarity; reposition subject and verb; tabulate. See answers, page 107.

1. The determination of proximate cause is usually a question of fact, including in cases of legal malpractice, but the determination of causation in those cases requires determining whether the appeal in the underlying action would have been successful but for the attorney's negligence.

2. Lawyers who are not in the same firm may divide fees only if the division is in proportion to the services provided or the client agrees and the lawyers assume joint responsibility for representation, the client is informed of the division, its terms, and the lawyers' participation and does not object, and the total fee is reasonable.

3. A lawyer cannot induce a client to make a substantial gift, e.g., money, property, stock, or future money, property, stock, etc., to the lawyer or the lawyer's parent, sibling, child, or spouse, except where the client is related to the attorney, but may accept a gift from the lawyer's client subject to general standards of fairness and absence of undue influence.

FRONT-LOADED SENTENCES

Sentences are "front-loaded" when the writer places long or complicated qualifying or descriptive information before the main subject and its verb. If you create these lopsided sentences, your readers will not understand the introductory, dependent material before they have a context for it; they'll have to read through it, hold all the dependent ideas in abeyance, and then find some way to incorporate those introductory words back into the sentence's main context.

> **✗** Given the absence of accurate and effective fines for disciplinary violations and an incentive on the part of lawyers to maximize overall gain by engaging in the unethical conduct, a **court**, faced with a choice between applying a narrow disciplinary rule such as the dishonesty rule, **will achieve** a more efficient result by adopting the narrower approach.

This sentence places 30 words *before* the beginning of the main clause—and the main subject (the court) is then *separated* by 15 more words from the sentence's active verb (will achieve). When you review your draft to sharpen your prose, make sure the main subjects of your sentences appear near the beginning where the reader expects them.

SOLUTIONS

1. **Break up** a front-loaded sentence into two sentences.

   No accurate and effective fines exist for disciplinary violations, plus lawyers have an incentive to maximize overall gain by engaging in the unethical conduct. **Thus, a court** will achieve a more efficient result by adopting the narrower approach, even when faced with a choice between applying a narrow disciplinary rule such as the dishonesty rule.

2. **Flip-flop** the sentence so that the main subject and verb are first.

   A **court will achieve** a more efficient result by adopting the narrower approach when it is faced with a choice between applying a narrow disciplinary rule such as the dishonesty rule, given the absence of accurate and effective fines for disciplinary violations and an incentive on the part of lawyers to maximize overall gain by engaging in the unethical conduct.

27

A bit of strategy: You may deliberately create a front-loaded sentence if you need to hide its true message.

| Try These |

Experiment with flip-flopping and then breaking apart these front-loaded sentences. Which of your rewrites reads more smoothly? See suggested answers, page 107.

1. Pursuant to a proposal from the Iowa Bar Association at the 1983 Midyear Meeting of the ABA House of Delegates, the words "fraudulent act" were deleted from the original 8.4(b), and language tracking Disciplinary Rule 1-102(A)(4) of the 1969 Code was inserted instead.

2. Although offensive to notions of aesthetic value and the sense that the Model Rules represent a coherent code, the mere presence of an anomaly is not necessarily poor public policy.

AWKWARD CITATION PLACEMENT

Citations are necessary, important, and generally compact; still, they can intrude on your legal issue and impede your reader's comprehension. Citations are important to document legal points. Do not, though, let their location in your sentences obscure your substantive message.

X *Office of Disciplinary Counsel v. Surrick,* 749 A.2d 441 (Penn. 2000), maintained that the decision should not apply to the defendant.

X The court held that scienter required by Rules of Professional Conduct 8.4(c) included reckless indifference to the trust. *Anonymous Attorney A,* 714 A.2d 402 (Penn. 1998).

2: CREATING SENTENCES WITH STYLE

Office of Disciplinary Counsel v. Surrick maintained that this decision should not apply to the defendant. *Office of Disciplinary Counsel v. Surrick*, 749 A.2d 441 (Penn. 2000).

SOLUTIONS

1. **Move** citations into prepositional phrases.

The Pennsylvania court, in *Office of Disciplinary Counsel v. Surrick*, 749 A.2d 441 (Penn. 2000), maintained that this decision should not apply to the defendant.

2. **Move** citations to the end of your sentence.

The Pennsylvania court maintained that this decision should not apply to the defendant. *Office of Disciplinary Counsel v. Surrick*, 749 A.2d 441 (Penn. 2000).

3. **Avoid** ending one sentence with a citation and beginning the next sentence with another citation.

A 1998 Pennsylvania court held that scienter required by Rules of Professional Conduct 8.4(c) included reckless indifference to the trust. *Anonymous Attorney A*, 714 A.2d 402 (Penn. 1998). Nevertheless, a 2000 Pennsylvania court maintained that this decision should not apply to the defendant. *Office of Disciplinary Counsel v. Surrick*, 749 A.2d 441 (Penn. 2000).

4. **Do not confuse** citation abbreviations with textual words. As the *ALWD Citation Manual* and *Harvard Manual on Style* explain, a citation used as a noun in a textual sentence is technically incorrect. The abbreviation is of course correct within a citation entry, but it is NOT correct as a noun within a sentence.[2]

---

[2] ALWD CITATION MANUAL RULE 2.3 (2nd Ed. 2003); THE BLUEBOOK: A UNIFORM SYSTEM OF CITATION RULE 10.2.1(c) (16th Ed. 1996).

This case is governed by RPC 8.4(c).

The Rules of Professional Conduct govern this case. RPC 8.4(c).

Try These

Move or correct the following citations using the above suggestions. See answers, page 108.

1. <u>Atkins v. Kirkpatrick</u>, 832 S.W.2d 547 (Tenn. Ct. App. 1991), set forth four standards necessary for "negligent misrepresentation."

2. Even though an attorney sanctioned under Rule 11 of the Federal Rules of Civil Procedure did not argue a false claim or frivolously pursue a material fact, <u>Hunter v. Earthgrains Co. Bakery</u>, 281 F.3d 144 (4th Cir. 2002), held the attorney guilty for advocating against the precedent of the Fourth Circuit, according to his defense lawyer, who maintains the court unfairly expanded Rule 11.

3. 29 U.S.C. §1399(b)(2)(A)(i) allows the employer to seek review of the schedule of payments; however, this dispute also falls under §1401, the arbitration provision.

TREACHEROUS PLACEMENT

Serious consequences develop in legal writing if a word can modify more than one antecedent (its "head word") and also if words aren't placed exactly where they need to be. When you examine your draft, concentrate on which words you intend to belong together as a unit, and which words you've misplaced where they might describe more than one noun.

 I have placed a newspaper ad for an honest lawyer and paralegal.

As written, the respondent to the ad must definitely be an honest lawyer; the writer **may also** require that the paralegal might need to be honest also. "May," however, is not precise enough for legal readers; precise modification is essential. Daily, courts are forced to interpret contract clauses with modifiers floating among several nouns; daily, lawyers argue over statutes and codes because the drafters did not precisely place the modifier.[3]

Legal writers, striving to produce precise prose, should also focus on a second problem with word placement: readers assume that modifiers will describe, delineate, or emphasize the word closest to them. And yet look at the readers' dilemma created below by a limiting modifier (almost, only, even, just):

He shot himself in the foot Monday.
Only **he** shot himself in the foot Monday.
He *only* **shot** himself in the foot Monday.
He shot *only* **himself** in the foot Monday.
He shot himself *only* **in the foot** Monday.
He shot himself in the foot *only* **Monday**.
He shot himself in the foot Monday *only*.

The second example of problematic word placement rises from the disjunctive nature of some adverbs (however, nevertheless, besides, still, meanwhile, instead). Again, though, their placement should emphasize the writer's intended emphasis or contrast.

If lawyers are paid to be rude and political consultants to be nasty, then professional athletes surely can brawl and bite the ears of their opponents. **After all**, athletes want to win too.

If lawyers are paid to be rude and political consultants to be nasty, then professional athletes surely can brawl and bite the ears of their opponents. Athletes, **after all**, want to win too.

---

[3] For examples of treacherous placement of words that have been litigated in court, see TERRI LECLERCQ, *Doctrine of the Last Antecedent*, 2 J. OF L. WRITING INSTITUTE 81.

If lawyers are paid to be rude and political consultants to be nasty, then professional athletes surely can brawl and bite the ears of their opponents. Athletes want to win too, **after all**.[4]

Each option emphasizes something different and is not wrong, but one placement may best suit your meaning.[5]

Misplaced phrases can also create ambiguity when they are used as modifiers:

 Jury members watched the judge making their decisions from quick impressions.

Jury members making their decisions from quick impressions watched the judge.

SOLUTIONS

1. **Place** modifiers precisely—directly before or directly after the word or word groups they modify.

2. **Evaluate** each modifier that might be interpreted to **modify more than one** noun.

 The candidate must pass the written test and the durability test within one week before beginning work. (**must** take durability test within a week; **might** also have to take written test within a week—but it's ambiguous)

Add Comma
The candidate must pass the written test and the durability test, within one week before beginning work. (must do both within one week)

---

[4] Original idea from STEPHEN CARTER, CIVILITY 284 (1998).
[5] Like "after all," the word "however" can be placed in any position to signal the writer's intended juxtaposition.

Move to Modify Full Clause
Within one week of beginning work, the candidate must pass the written test and the durability test. (must do both within one week)

3. **Break the sentence** into two or add additional limitations to the antecedents if you intend the modifier to limit only one noun.

Break into Two Sentences
The candidate must, within one week before beginning work, pass the written test. He also must pass the durability test.

Separate Antecedents and Add "Also," etc.
The candidate must pass the written test within one week before beginning work, and he should also pass the durability test.

4. **Review** your drafts slowly and systematically, searching for any sentence in which your modifiers could have misinterpreted antecedents.

Try These

Examine the placement of modifiers in these sentences. If they are misplaced or ambiguous, correct them. If they represent two or more interpretations, be prepared to explain those possibilities. See answers, page 108.

1. Robin Mayhem tried "at least ten times" to leave Jamail Fenwick, father of her two baby boys, who she said would beat her regularly.

2. The rule, with all its attendant enforcement costs, only results in a marginal reduction in instances of unethical conduct.

3. After receiving the client's money, you must deposit the check and have it listed as a separate account within two weeks of receipt.

FAULTY PARALLELISM

Parallel ideas are often conveyed forcefully through parallel grammatical structures. Verbs can be parallel, as can nouns, adjectives—indeed, full sentences. When a writer gets these parallels correct, the parallel structures frequently produce persuasive, memorable prose.

> Say that the plaintiff was driving too slowly. Say that she did not use her car's signal lights. But you cannot say that she broke a law.

Still, misuse of parallelism can create confusion. Writers most frequently have trouble with parallelism if they do not check to see that each item in a series or list is grammatically the same, that is, parallel in syntactic structure. A second problem is a list with an introductory word or phrase that is later *repeated*. Or, a writer can lose that parallel because a signal is *missing* that would pinpoint what items are parallel.

Repeated introductory word:

> **X** The dishonesty rule represents poor policy, is open to constitutional challenge, and it violates due process. ("it" repeats the introductory noun "rule")

Missing signal for parallel list:

> **X** The state bar committee has helped the image of attorneys by not allowing dishonest attorneys to practice, publicizing pro bono activities, and educating members of the bar about professional conduct. ("by not allowing," "by publicizing," and "by educating")

S O L U T I O N S

1. Keep **syntactically equal** items parallel.

> Koby's interaction with the Human Rights Commission included **creating an inventory** of past issues and **assistance** about current European cases.

34

Koby's interaction with the Human Rights Commission included **creating an inventory** of past issues and **assisting with** current European cases.

2. Review your **numbered lists,** which highlight grammatically parallel items.

   X Other provisions of Section 6 provide (1) **for** the requisites of the application for a bondsman's license, (2) **for** an investigation and hearing by the board, and (3) **its denial** of the application or approval conditioned on the applicant's filing of the required security deposit.

   Other provisions of Section 6 provide (1) **for** the requisites of the application for a bondsman's license, (2) **for** an investigation and hearing by the board, and (3) **for** its denial of the application or approval conditioned on the applicant's filing of the required security deposit.

3. Keep **signals** apparent to reflect parallel items.

   X Thus, the court held **that** the complaint was not vague or conclusory **and it** was "adequate to give notice of the claims asserted."

   Thus, the court held **that** the complaint was not vague or conclusory and **that** it was "adequate to give notice of the claims asserted."

4. Keep items parallel that follow **correlative conjunctions**.

   | either . . . or |
   | neither . . . nor |
   | both . . . and |
   | not only . . . but also |
   | whether . . . or |

   The attorney paid attention **not only** to the witness **but also** to her earlier deposition statements.

   X **Not only** were the first-year students afraid of the new professors **but also** their classmates. (emphasizes **were the first-year students**)

35

The freshman students were afraid **not only** of the new professors **but also** of their classmates.

5. Avoid losing parallelism with **an inadvertent repetition** of "that" in a string of clauses.

 He said **that** because he was going to file before June **that** the statute of limitations would not have run.

He said that, because he was going to file before June, the statute of limitations would not have run.

Try These

Redo these sentences as necessary to create parallel items within them. See answers, page 109.

1. The doctrine of unconstitutional vagueness provides (1) for adequate notice of a rule and (2) is a safeguard against governmental abuse.

2. The plaintiff must show:

   a. a reasonable probability that the parties would enter into a contractual relationship;

   b. that the defendant acted maliciously by intentionally preventing the relationship from occurring with the purpose of harming the plaintiff;

   c. in addition to not being privileged, that the defendant was not justified; and

   d. actual harm or damage occurred as a result of the interference.

3. A lawyer may not engage in dishonesty, fraud, deceit, misrepresentation, or give false statements.

PASSIVE VOICE

We've all been taught to avoid the passive voice, but a rare few of us remember what it is. A quick review: a verb is "active" when the subject of the sentence is performing the action: "The court held that the defendant was negligent." But if the subject is acted upon by something else (as this very clause demonstrates), the verb is "passive":[6]

The plaintiff was injured by the vehicle.

Overuse or inadvertent use of the passive voice causes several problems:

- The passive adds unnecessary words.
- The passive steals the punch from strong, active verbs.
- The passive can create ambiguity (truncated passive).
- The passive can misplace sentence emphasis.

Adding unnecessary words:

 The term "cosmic detachment" **is used by** Richard Wydick to explain abstract legal style. (14 words)

Richard Wydick **describes** abstract legal style as "cosmic detachment." (9 words)

Stealing the punch from strong, active verbs:

 The plaintiff **was** severely **hurt** by the defendant's car.

---

[6] Students might confuse the passive voice with a past tense: *The attorney had defended this client. (not passive, merely past perfect tense).* Other writers confuse "to be," used as a linking verb, with the passive voice: *Clark and Lois are preparing today's brief. (active, linking verb—not a passive).* Even the passive voice can have several tenses: *The campaign is being run by the Democrats at Large. (passive, present progressive); The unsuspecting client was hit by an enormous bill. (passive, past tense).* Remember that although the passive voice always includes a form of the "to be" verb, not all "to be" verbs are passive.

The defendant's car **crippled** (paralyzed, injured) the plaintiff.

Adding ambiguity: truncated passives (person/agent missing):

X The pedestrian **was hit** twice. (The subject (pedestrian) did not perform the action (hit) and the verb has no direct object, so the sentence is truncated.)

The defendant's car **hit** the pedestrian twice. (The subject (car) did the hitting.)

Gerry Jones, defendant, **hit** the pedestrian twice with his car. (Gerry Jones did the hitting.)

Misplacing emphasis:

X In Jabrowski the defendant's plane **was flown** low over the plaintiff's land during the crop-dusting operation. (Who did what to whom?)

In Jabrowski the **pilot flew** his plane low over the plaintiff's land during the crop-dusting operation. (The pilot flew over land.)

Artful use of passive voice:

The passive voice can be used deliberately:

- when you *do not know* the agent/actor.
    The girl was propelled out of the train.
- when you need to *protect* your "subject" from a direct accusation.
    Marta was dismissed from law school.
- when you want to *emphasize the result* of an action.
    George was murdered by a drunken driver.

Try These

Switch the following passive constructions into the active voice. See answers, page 109.

1. The modern origins of the dishonesty rule may be found in the 1908 American Bar Association (ABA) Canons of Professional Ethics.

2. It was held by the committee, for example, that a lawyer violates the dishonesty rule if he assists a litigant who purports to appear *pro se*, but the litigant fails to notify the court that he is receiving the advice of counsel.

3. The law would not be struck as unconstitutionally vague if it were capable of being made reasonably clear through judicial interpretation.

LENGTHY QUOTATIONS

Legal writing is filled with quoted material that interrupts the flow of the text. Yes, our legal system is built on stare decisis and depends on precedent, and, yes, the reader needs to know your source. But as you review your draft, evaluate **how much** precedent you've directly quoted and **why**. Was each word of each case that you've quoted within your draft essential? Or were you rushed for time? Was the language too complicated for you to paraphrase?

Huge blocks of quoted information cannot logically address **your** main point. If you include a long block quotation, you cannot simultaneously explain how all of its points fit together with your case. Instead, you may notice that you resort to underlining the essential language within the long quotation or to pulling out the essential language in the discussion that follows the block quotation.

A second common writing problem that creates confusion for the reader is a quotation stuck into the discussion with no introduction. If the writer were to briefly introduce the quotation, perhaps using a sentence that gives the gist of the following material, then readers would have a context before reading and might even understand where their attention should be. Examine the following paragraph, part of a court's argument, and see effective word quotations, paraphrases, and block quotations:

paraphrase, then ▶ direct quotation incorporated into text	Mazuca was clearly negligent. Whether he acted conscionably is less certain. Attorneys can be found to be engaged in unconscionable conduct "by the way they represent their clients." <u>Latham v. Castillo</u>, 972 S.W.2d 66, 68 (Tex. 1998). However, given the likelihood that personal jurisdiction was not a possibility over Nuzum in Texas, Mazuca's decision to nonsuit the Texas case in favor of mediation, which could have settled the case, does not fit the description of unconscionability. Because the nonsuit was filed without prejudice, he could have filed it at any time before the statute ran.
brief introduction ▶	"Unconscionable" is defined under the DTPA to mean an act or practice that:
direct language of ▶ Act necessary	(a) takes advantage or the lack of knowledge, ability, experience, or capacity of a person to a grossly unfair degree; or (b) results in a gross disparity between the value received and consideration paid, in a transaction involving transfer of consideration.
paraphrase ▶	<u>Tex. Bus. & Com. Code Ann.</u> §§ 17.45(5) Vernon (1987). The 1995 amendments to the DTPA allow an attorney to be held liable for an unconscionable action or course of action that cannot be characterized as advice, judgment, or opinion. <u>Tex. Bus. & Com. Code</u>

quoted language ▶
integrated into text

another direct ▶
quotation from case
follows a transition
from text

Ann. §§ 17.49(c)(3). The amendments further require a showing that the resulting infairness was "glaringly noticeable, flagrant, complete, and unmitigated. . . ." Chastain v. Koonce, 700 S.W.2d 579, 584 (Tex. 1985). In contrast, "[a] claim based upon the failure to exercise that degree of care, skill, and diligence that a lawyer of ordinary skill and knowledge commonly possesses and exercises, despite its label, is a malpractice claim." Kahlig v. Boyd, 980 S.W.2d 685, 689 (Tex. App.-San Antonio 1998).[7]

The information below offers writers both the pros and cons of three methods for incorporating text into their discussion.

Long block quotations:

Pro

- add validity through stark presentation of language
- stand out on the page
- can highlight extended controversial/colorful language

Con

- are easily skipped by hurried readers
- can be difficult to integrate into a writer's textual point
- can introduce extraneous material and even contradict the writer's intended point
- can create a black, dense look to a document
- can be interpreted as sloppy writing
- need an especially strong introductory tag line and conclusion in the writer's text
- reproduce poorly written prose of the original writer whose point is useful but whose prose is deadly

---

[7] Modified from Mazuca v. Schumann, 82 S.W.3d 90, 94.

Shorter word/phrase quotations:

Pro

- integrate more easily into the writer's text
- will keep the readers' focus on the writer's analysis rather than on case summaries
- allow a writer to retain colorful and controversial language that readers could find persuasive

Con

- if used out of context, can destroy credibility

Paraphrasing:

Pro

- most successfully integrates outside information into a writer's own text
- creates shorter, smoother documents

Con

- requires the writer to be more sophisticated with, and take more care to provide, careful signals
- should not be used when the exact wording is in dispute
- can fail if signals indicating who/said/what are too weak for readers to follow
- can confuse readers if writer quotes more than one source within a sentence

After you've edited your draft's organization (with its thesis, road map, and headings), investigate your sentence-level prose: sentence length and order, passives and left-handed sentences, parallel structures, and placement of citations. As you read through your draft this time, review each sentence merely as a sentence—and not as an information-carrier. This technique allows you to see your writing as your reader does: sentence by sentence. The time you expend tightening each sentence will eventually pay off by giving you credibility with your reader.

What to Remember

After you've finished your draft and returned to it to revise your organization, then you need to take another step: read your draft, last sentence first, and revise any incorrect or obstructive sentence structure. Beginning with the last sentence allows you to see the sentence merely as an information-deliverer, not as a piece of the paragraph's logic. Focusing strictly on sentences, investigate your sentence length and order, passives and front-loaded sentences, parallel structures, and the placement of citations. Tightening your sentences will also reduce the length of your document.

CONCLUDING EXERCISES

First identify the stylistic error that each sentence represents. Then edit it for readability. See answers, page 110.

1. If there is a reasonable prospect that disclosing or using confidential client information will adversely affect a material interest of the client or if the client has instructed the lawyer not to use or disclose the information, then it is a lawyer's duty to safeguard that information.

2. Commentators have recognized an attorney's negligence during trial and its preparation as a question of law.

> Initially, the client must prove that, but for the attorney's negligence, the plaintiff should have prevailed upon the motion or appeal. . . . The decision about the proper resolution of a petition or appeal must and can be made by the trial judge *as an issue of law*, based upon review of the transcript and record of the underlying action, the argument of counsel, and subject to the same rules of

review as should have been applied [by the appellate court] to the motion or appeal.

2 R. Mallen & J. Smith, Legal Malpractice §§ 24.39, at 536-37 (3d ed. 1989) [emphasis added].

3. All funds received for the benefit of clients should be deposited in an identifiable bank account labeled "Trust Account" or words of similar import.

4. By presenting to the court a pleading, motion, or other paper, an attorney or unrepresented party is certifying to the best of the person's knowledge, information, and belief, formed after an inquiry reasonable under the circumstances, that it is not being presented for any improper purpose, and other legal contentions therein are warranted by existing law, and that the allegations and other factual contentions have evidentiary support or, if specifically so identified, are likely to have evidentiary support after a reasonable opportunity for further investigation or discovery, and that the denials of factual contentions are warranted on the evidence, or, if specifically so identified, are reasonably based on a lack of information or belief.

5. An attorney cannot deposit funds belonging to a member of a law firm into a client's Trust account unless they are funds to pay reasonable bank charges or if the client and firm member have collectively added the money to the account, then the law firm member must withdraw his/her amount as soon as possible.

6. You may not solicit a client from your previous law firm without that firm's written contract provision or permission.

7. That a lawyer engages in conduct that may be contrary to the Rules of Professional Conduct does not automatically give rise to

a civil cause of action. *Noble v. Sears, Roebuck & Co,* 33 Cal. App. 3d 654 (1973). *Klemm v. Superior Court,* 75 Cal. App. 3d 893 (1977), held, however, that the disciplinary rules are not intended to supercede existing law relating to lawyers in non-disciplinary contexts.

♦ ♦ ♦

There are only two cures for the long sentence: (1) Say less; (2) Put a period in the middle. Neither expedient has taken hold in the law.
DAVID MELLINKOFF, THE LANGUAGE OF THE LAW 366 (1963)

♦ ♦ ♦

3

CHOOSING WORDS WITH STYLE

Precise word choice can mean the difference between success and failure. This chapter advises you to look, once again, at your draft to ensure that it says exactly what you intended.

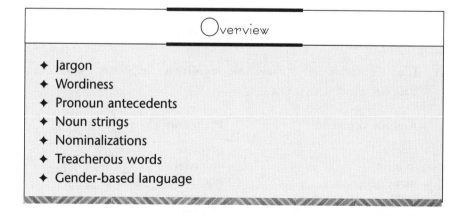

Overview

+ Jargon
+ Wordiness
+ Pronoun antecedents
+ Noun strings
+ Nominalizations
+ Treacherous words
+ Gender-based language

JARGON

Every profession has its share of **jargon**, that specialized vocabulary used within a group with common backgrounds or interests. The use of jargon can save time—and imply an insider's connection. Newspapermen "put the issue to bed," and students sign up for classes on "M-W-F or T-T." This jargon is understood by everyone within that group but can baffle those outside it.

Terms of art, on the other hand, are a shorthand to underlying concepts. Attorneys depend on terms of art for daily communication among themselves: *dictum, garnishment, fee simple.* Readers untrained in the law cannot be expected to understand these terms, and, interestingly, many specialized words within one area of law confuse even other lawyers. For instance, home insurance policies can bewilder antitrust lawyers.

Legal writers inadvertently slip these specialized words and phrases into documents for laymen because they forget that others aren't familiar with them. Jargon, then, is a matter of **audience**. The needs of your audience must be met in each choice of word, just as they were met within your choices for organization and sentence structure. Your goal will be to craft an understandable discussion for your anticipated audience: your professor on an exam; the judge or your classmates; your client, who may or may not have a legal background.

S O L U T I O N S

1. Identify and weed out **archaic legalisms,** i.e., words with plain English equivalents:

Archaic Legalism	Plain English
aforesaid	previous
forthwith	immediately
henceforth	from now on
herein	in this document
hereinafter	after this

thenceforth	after
thereafter	after that, accordingly
therein	in
theretofore	up to that time
hitherto	before
viz.	that is, *or* for example
whence	from what place, source
whereby	through, in accordance
said	the, that
whilst	during

2. Recognize **coupled synonyms**, which were useful hundreds of years ago when three languages (French, Latin, and versions of Old English) were used simultaneously on one English island. Replace them, when practical,[1] with one term your reader will understand. For instance, instead of repeating "each and every," use only "each":

Coupled Synonyms

acknowledge and confess	act and deed
aid and abet	annul and set aside
authorize and empower	absolutely and completely
covenant and surmise	deem and consider
covenant and agree	each and every
due and payable	each and all
excess and unnecessary	false and untrue
final and conclusive	full and complete
fit and proper	have and hold
for and in consideration of	force and effect
fraud and deceit	in truth and in fact
in my stead and place	from and after
free and unfettered	let or hindrance
for and during	for and in consideration of
give, devise, and bequeath	keep and maintain
last will and testament	truth and veracity
lot, tract, or parcel of land	modified or changed

---

[1] Be careful not to throw out necessary legal terms! For instance, "ready, willing, and able" are not legally redundant. Someone could be *willing* to share a document but not *ready* because the document has not been located. See TERRI LeCLERCQ, *Jargon: Manure, Margarine, and Moderation*, EXPERT LEGAL WRITING 119, 122 (1995).

null, void, and of no effect	order and direct
ordered, judged, and decreed	save and except
type and kind	void and of no effect

3. **Eliminate** unnecessary, **overused legal phrases** that are a part of jargon and **replace** them with concrete references to a case name, the parties' names, and specific pronouns.

Overused	**Suggested Replacements**
in this instant case	in this case, here (or use parties' names)
one must prove	the defendant must prove (or use name)
the court below	the trial [district] court
the said party	that party, the plaintiff [defendant]

Try These

Find common terminology and shorter phrases to replace the following jargon. See answers, page 111.

1. Attorney Don Miller refutes this charge. The said party contends also that he has been unfairly enjoined into this suit.

2. She alleges violation of certain state law claims, to wit: fraud, breach of contract, and misrepresentation.

WORDINESS

Legal documents frequently read as if the office copier has accidentally duplicated previous paragraphs. Because repetition results in lengthy documents and uninteresting reading, focus on your drafts with a hungry eye. Imagine how much more forceful your prose will be if you **cut a fourth** from your draft.

Solutions

1. Omit unnecessary **prepositions**.

    She consulted **with** her attorney **in regard to** an accident. (10 words)

   She consulted her attorney **about** an accident. (7 words)

    The **language of the statute** will not explicitly tell you what the legislature intended. (14 words)

   The **statute's language** will not explicitly tell you the legislature's intention. (11 words)

2. Replace unnecessary or ambiguous **passive voice** verbs. (*See also* Chapter 2.)

    It was held by the court that the attorney was guilty of professional neglect. (14 words)

   The court held the attorney guilty of professional neglect. (9 words)

    Confidential information about a client cannot **be revealed** without consent. (10 words, ambiguous)

   An attorney **may not reveal** confidential information about a client unless **the client consents**. (14 words, but precise)

3. Omit unnecessary **relative pronouns**.

    He was the man **who** knocked on your door. (9 words)

   He knocked on your door. (5 words)

He said **that** it was a problem **that** he would look into.[2] (12 words)

He said he would look into the problem. (8 words)

4. Omit **throat-clearers.**

✗	obviously	✗	clearly
✗	manifestly	✗	case is when
✗	as a matter of fact	✗	to tell the truth
✗	it is obvious that	✗	it is clear
✗	case is when	✗	situation is where
✗	it would appear to be the case that		

 It is interesting that attorney malpractice rules have changed so slowly. (11 words)

Attorney malpractice rules have changed slowly. (6 words)

 The **kind of** issue in these circumstances is probable cause. (10 words)

The issue in these circumstances is probable cause. (8 words)

5. Replace **unnecessary expletives**, e.g., "there is," "there are," and "it is."[3]

 There is no other method, except by deposition, by which Black can obtain this material. (15 words)

---

[2] There is no iron-clad rule about the inclusion of "that," so common sense will have to tell you when you have used too many, or when, because you've omitted the "that," you have lost the coherence that a relative pronoun provided.

[3] Some sentences may need to begin with "there is": "There is reason to worry today." It is clumsy and even wordier to revise this expletive into "A reason to worry today exists."

Black cannot obtain this material except by deposition. (8 words)

 It is important **that** fathers should continue to pay child support if the child chooses to attend college, even though the child is over the age of 18. (28 words)

Fathers should continue to pay child support if the child chooses to attend college, even though the child is over 18. (21 words)

6. Avoid **unnecessary modification** unless it serves a tactical purpose.

 The second defendant is plainly and unequivocally innocent. (8 words)

The second defendant is innocent. (5 words)

7. Watch for **redundancy**.

Redundant	**Possible Revision**
✗ alleged suspect	suspect
✗ consensus of opinion	consensus
✗ free gift	gift
✗ rather (or most) unique	unique
✗ the said party	that party, the defendants
✗ whether or not[4]	
✗ next subsequent	subsequent
✗ personal (or honest) opinion	opinion
✗ single most	most
✗ reason is because	reason is (*or* because)

---

[4] "Whether or not" is usually redundant: *We do not know* **whether or not** *the executive summary will bring you immediate benefits (unnecessary "or not"*). But like most "rules," this one does not cover all possibilities: *Agency fees are collected to defray expenses of the activities of the union, expenses that benefit all members of the collective bargaining unit,* **whether union members or not.** Here the "or not" is syntactically necessary to complete the thought.

X The **holding** of *In re Gatti,* 8 P.3d 966 (Or. 2000), **held** that when a rule contains a number of specific exceptions, courts will likely read those exceptions as exclusive and refuse to create additional judicial exceptions.

In re Gatti, 8 P.3d 966 (Or. 2000), **held** that when a rule contains a number of specific exceptions, courts will likely read those exceptions as exclusive and refuse to create additional judicial exceptions.

Try These

Which of these phrases and sentences can be shortened and yet not substantially changed? See answers, page 112.

1. for the purpose of evaluating

2. went on to say that

3. The obligation of the attorney may have existed in a moral way, but not in a legal way.

PRONOUN ANTECEDENTS

If a sentence containing a pronoun has more than one possible antecedent (noun) or if the antecedent is left unstated, then the reader is left wondering who did what with whom.

Detective Miller's counsel did not cross-examine Sharlot in the presence of the jury and now contends, as he did on direct appeal, that by not being able to go into Sharlot's background, **he** was prevented from showing **his** bias or prejudice for testifying as **he** did, in violation of **his** Sixth Amendment right to confrontation. [Who is "he, " "his," or "him"?]

S O L U T I O N S

1. Beware of **multiple antecedents**.[5]

✗ Because he was screaming abuses, the defendant ordered the police officer to arrest the man. [Who was screaming: The defendant? The police officer? The man? We need the pronoun attached to or replaced by one of the nouns for clarity.]

2. Be specific with **relative** and **demonstrative** pronouns.

Demonstrative Pronouns	Relative Pronouns
this	who, whom
that	that, which
these	what, whatever
	whomever, whoever
	whichever

✗ The Model Code of Responsibility says a lawyer may not "threaten to present criminal charges solely to obtain an advantage in a civil matter." DR 7-105. **This** would focus lawyers for both sides on the actual issue. [Here, "this" demonstrative pronoun does not have a specific antecedent and is thus ambiguous. Follow it with a concrete noun: "this limitation" or "this restriction."]

✗ A lawyer may not "threaten to present criminal charges solely to obtain an advantage in a civil matter," **which** keeps lawyers on both sides focused on the issue. [Here, "which" has no concrete antecedent and is thus ambiguous. Rewrite the phrase: ... civil matter," a limitation that keeps or ... civil matter"; that limitation keeps.]

---

[5] See also Chapter 2, Treacherous Placement.

┌─────────────────────────────────────┐
│   Try These   │
└─────────────────────────────────────┘

Rewrite the following sentences, replacing ambiguous pronouns and limiting the antecedent that a pronoun can refer to. See answers, page 112.

1. The question is whether Smith informed others of the defect in the computer board design and if this caused the loss of benefits Dell expected from these companies.

2. If there are cases on point with similar fact situations and you are discussing an issue that calls for argument, these will give more weight to your argument.

3. A lawyer is subject to discipline if he makes a materially false statement in, or fails to disclose a material fact in connection with, application to the bar. Law school career service offices attempt to publicize them.

NOUN STRINGS

Noun strings make legal writing dense and difficult. In a noun string, a succession of nouns modify each other; thus each preceding noun functions as an adjective that modifies the last noun:

He believed he had a <u>good</u> <u>faith</u> <u>exception</u> for his behavior.

modifier modifier noun

Until readers locate the noun (exception), they must assume that each noun **functions** as a noun. After reading "good" and "faith," readers naturally assume the noun subject is "faith." Then they waste time and patience reprocessing those nouns into adjectives.

Noun strings camouflage the logical relationship between the nouns, and between the nouns and any adjective that may precede them. Here is an example that cost a building contractor his job: someone called, asking the contractor to send a number of support bars to a construction site. Over the phone, the buyer asked,

"Tomorrow morning, will you deliver ten, foot-long concrete bars?" The contractor agreed and wrote on the order "ten foot long concrete bars" plus the address, etc. The next morning, the loading team arrived with bars—bars that the buyer refused. Why? Look at the difference between these terms, and imagine the confused result:

- ten foot-long concrete bars
- ten-foot-long concrete bars

The error cost both time and supplies—and thus the contractor's job.

SOLUTIONS

1. Add a **hyphen** to connect two or more of the adjectives.

    low-interest real estate loans
    one-time tax write off

2. **Unstring** the noun string.

     a gross receipt sales tax

    - a gross-receipt sales tax
    - a sales tax on gross receipts

     new financial institutions franchises

    - new financial-institutions franchises
    - franchises for new financial institutions

Try These

Separate nouns and add connecting words or hyphens as necessary. Which terms are so ambiguous that the writer's intent cannot be determined? See answers, page 112.

1. certified return receipt postcard

2. funded welfare insurance programs

3. the bank's credit review service

NOMINALIZATIONS

Many a strong verb or concrete noun is hidden beneath a **nominalization**, those multisyllabic words with Latinate suffixes and prefixes such as -ize, -osity, -ate, -ability, -tion, -ancy, -ion, -al, -ence, -ive, -ment, de-, and mis- (examples: investiga**tion**, necessit**ate**, intelli-**gence, mis**appropriate). Although grammatically correct, nominalizations dilute a sentence by implying, rather than stating, the logical who/what relationships in the sentence.

 We made an **investigation** before we deposed the witness.

We **investigated** before deposing the witness.

 Despite the lawyer's **protestations**, the state bar committee held him in contempt.

Although the lawyer **protested**, the state bar committee held him in contempt.

Solutions

1. Watch for and replace nouns created **from verbs:**

Nominalization	Verb Form
determination	to determine
resolution	to resolve
utilization	to use
reinforcement	to enforce
the addition of	to add

58

assumption	to assume
continuation	to continue

2. Also watch for and replace nouns created from **adjectives** (that were themselves once verbs):

Noun/Adjective	Original Verb
enforceability/enforceable	enforce
applicability/applicable	apply
specificity/specific	specify

A good check for your draft is to read each sentence separately, applying the "who / did what / to whom?" test.

$$\boxed{\text{Try These}}$$

Identify any nominalizations, and rewrite to clarify the who / did what / to whom action that has been implied. See answers, page 113.

1. After thorough investigation of your deposition files, we offer the suggestion that you create new coding.

2. Thank you for allowing our firm to make our presentation of international issues in relationship to your business.

TREACHEROUS WORDS

A serious task for legal writers is choosing the exact and necessary word. Some words elude us as we draft; others sound correct in a context but aren't; some words are incorrect in any context. No one knows the meaning of every word or when to use each word he or she does know. But in legal writing, it is essential to review the shades of difference between synonyms, for instance, and to keep track of those words you frequently misuse.

Textual ambiguity:

 This is a key element in *Lopez* **which** distinguishes it from other Commerce Clause case law.

Interpretation 1. The writer intended to emphasize only the key element of <u>*Lopez*</u>, so she needed a comma after *Lopez*.

Interpretation 2. The writer intended to point out that the key element distinguishes it from case law and thus should have replaced the "which" with "that" to signal an essential and necessary clause. See also Chapter 2, that/which.

Unexpected repetition:

 The court's **holding** in <u>Katzenbach v. Morgan</u>, 384 U.S. 641 (1966), **held** that Section 4(e) of the 1965 Voting Rights Act was appropriate legislation to enforce the Equal Protection Clause.

See also Wordiness: Redundancy.

Misused words:

1. affect/effect: *Affect* is a verb, meaning to influence or to assume the appearance of. *Effect* is a noun, meaning the result. *Effect* can also be a verb meaning "to make a change" or "to accomplish."

2. alternative/option, choice: If you have *two* choices, each is an *alternative* to the other. Traditionally, linguists have held that with more than two options, you have *options* or *choices* but not an *alternative*. Contemporary linguists no longer hold tightly to this distinction.

3. among/between: *Among* refers to groups of three and more; *between* functions as a distinction between only two things. (*Among* the many functions of the teaching assistants is the chore of arranging all social functions. *Between* class assignments and work with the freshmen, the teaching assistants have little extra time.)

Between and *among* require objective pronouns: Between you and *me*, I can't stand to witness fights between *him* and *her*. Among *us*, the custom is to bring cookies to the study group once a week.

4. as/because: *As* is a comparative, like *like*. Tradition and preciseness limits *because* as a signal for causality.

> Incorrect: *As* he was slow to file all court documents, the committee disqualified him.
> Correct: *Because* he was slow to file all court documents, the committee disqualified him.
> Correct: The Plaintiff can be *as* sincere *as* a nun, but *because* she has her dates wrong, she will not be believed.

5. assure/insure/ensure: All three of these words mean to make certain or safe, so their precise use is complicated. You *assure* people (removing doubt and suspense). You *insure* with money and guarantees and (insurance) policies. And you *ensure* when you are making a thing certain or safe, e.g., *ensure* your child's safety with a seat belt.

6. assume/presume: To *assume* is to take for granted that something is true or accurate. To *presume* is to take upon oneself without leave or warrant, to dare or go beyond what is right or proper. Perhaps you can remember the difference by noting the use of the root in *presumption*.

7. because/since: Traditionally, these words signaled different meanings and were not interchangeable. Although it is not technically incorrect to use them interchangeably now, it will benefit a legal writer to limit *since* to signal time, and *because* to signal causality.

8. bimonthly/semimonthly: Enough confusion exists about these words that most writers resort to using "every two months" or "twice a month." *Bi* means two; *semi* means half. Thus, *bimonthly* is every two months, and *semimonthly* is twice a month.

9. continuous/continual: *Continuous* means occurring without interference; *continual* means frequently occurring. The professor gave a two-hour, *continuous* lecture. A disgruntled student in the back row offered *continual* interruptions.

10. composed/comprised: *Composed* means to be made of (the parts compose the whole), and *comprised* means contains (the whole comprises the parts). The audience is *composed of* people with varied backgrounds. The symphony hall *comprises* people with varied backgrounds.

11. currently/presently: Although the nouns *current* and *present* are basically synonymous, the adverb forms traditionally signal a difference in time. We are *currently* (right now) studying word choice. *Presently* (in the very near future) we will stop and take a break.

12. different than/different from: Things *differ from* each other. *Different than* is considered incorrect unless the preferred form creates bulky, illogical phraseology following it.

Black's argument is *different from* White's.

I agree that the Supreme Court has interpreted the United States Constitution very *differently than* the Founders intended and that courts err on the side of tyranny. (A rewrite to replace "differently than" would be awkward: "I agree that the Supreme Court has interpreted the United States Constitution differently from the way that the Founders intended and that courts err on the side of tyranny.")

13. discreet/discrete: A *discreet* investigator is tactful and judicious, careful. An investigator may be *discrete* from other witnesses at the trial, meaning that he is disconnected from them, separate and distinct.

14. disinterested/uninterested: These words are surprisingly different. A judge or stenographer is *disinterested* in a case; that is, the judge has no personal involvement in it and yet needs to know the details of the case. The court clerk may truly be *uninterested*, that is, not engaged by the elements of the story. Because the child was totally *uninterested* in the legal proceeding, she fell asleep.

15. historic/historical: A *historic* occasion is momentous, one that will make history. If the event already belongs in the past, it is *historical*, as are historical novels that thus deal with past events. (A side issue here is "*a* historic" versus "*an* historic." In America, we sound out our *h*'s. So unless you are willing to consistently write "an hot date" or "an historical moment," you need to use an *a* before *historic*.)

16. i.e./e.g.: *I.e.*, an abbreviation of *id est*, means "that is" and indicates that an inclusive list or statement will follow. On the other hand, *e.g.*, (*exempli gratia*) means "for example" and signals that the author is including an example or examples with the introductory statement.

I like literature; *i.e.*, I read everything I can get my hands on.
I like literature; *e.g.*, I am reading all of Anne Tyler this month.

17. imply/infer: To *imply* is to hint at something. To *infer* is to suggest an intimate or incriminating connection.

He *implied* that she was not telling the truth when he asked to see her list of references.

He *inferred* that his client was angry because she never looked directly at him across the table.

18. it's/its: *It's* easy to distinguish these two forms if you can remember that the apostrophe signals that a letter is left out, so the form *it's* must stand for "it is." Following that rule will force its competitor, *its*, into its only logical slot, as a third-person singular pronoun.

19. lay/lie: *Lay* means to place or put and usually takes an object (transitive verb). Past tense: laid. Perfect: laid. *Lie* means recline (intransitive verb). Past tense: lay. Perfect: lain. She *laid* her casebooks on the table. He *lay* awake all night before the exam.

20. prescribe/proscribe: You *prescribe* when you are giving a remedy or a decree. The opposite is true of *proscribe*, when you are forbidding, prohibiting.

21. reluctant/reticent: If your witness is *reluctant* to testify, she is unwilling or will grudgingly consent. That she is *reticent*, however, means she does not reveal her feelings readily.

22. that/which: If you draft an essential (restrictive) clause that will not be punctuated "out" of the sentence with commas, use *that*. If the clause is meant to be nonessential, relatively unnecessary to the sentence's meaning, use two commas and *which*.

The clause *that* you need the most is not punctuated.

The clause, *which* is not essential to the sentence, disappeared from the eye when it was set off with commas.

23. who/which: If your antecedent is inanimate (nonhuman), use *that* or *which* as a pronoun. If the antecedent is a person, use *who*. The question becomes more complicated when you are referring, for instance, to an agency filled with people. If you are referring to the agency as a whole, use *which*; if the people within the agency are the center of your sentence or its intent, use *who* and *whom*.

Correct: The factfinders of the agency, *who* are veteran questioners, believe the client has previous fraudulent claims.

Correct: The initiating agency, *which* inquired about the status of our jurisdiction, has been satisfied through an earlier memorandum.

Incorrect: Grades are a tag and weight fastened on you by the faculty, *which* determine exactly how high in the legal world you are going to rise at graduation. (Like any relative or demonstrative pronoun, *which* should refer to the closest logical antecedent. Perhaps here the antecedent is "faculty," but the plural verb "determine" indicates that the intended subjects are "tag and weight.")

SOLUTIONS

1. Consult **professional sources** like Wilson Follett, *Modern American Usage: A Guide*; W.H. Fowler, *A Dictionary of Modern English Usage*; David Mellinkoff, *Mellinkoff's Dictionary of American Legal Usage*. Using them, **study** those words frequently misused.

2. Create **your own list** of words that confuse you or that you frequently misuse. Keep the list in your computer thesaurus or on a list near your writing area.

Try These

Investigate the word choice in these examples. Eliminate repetitions and edit for ambiguous or misused words. See answers, page 113.

1. As the clerk had stood to attention, the court audience did also.

2. Attorney Fred Fudd recommended that Mrs. Baker hire someone to monitor her work and insure that premiums were properly dispersed.

3. The therapist posited various possible causes for the child's anxiety, i.e., travel between two households, parental inability to communicate, participating in contrasting religious activities, etc.

GENDER-BASED LANGUAGE

Historically, the English language used masculine **nouns** as generic placeholders for both genders (man<u>kind</u>, fire<u>man</u>). Similarly, English has a tradition that gender-based **pronouns** reflect both genders. (An attorney should call <u>his</u> office.) Today, however, linguists and psychologists have made us aware of the subliminal impact that this historical tradition has had on our society,[6] and the law's role in the perpetuation of that impact.

Perhaps, someday, someone will invent a new third-person pronoun with no gender implications. Right now, though, legal stylists can avoid limiting society to its masculine components through the following alternatives.

SOLUTIONS

1. Switch your sentence to the **third person plural, unless the change creates ambiguity:**

 A judge requires his clerks to work late.

Judges expect their clerks to work late.

 Each of the clerks decided they would bring their pillows from home. ("Each" is a singular noun requiring a singular pronoun.)

All of the clerks decided they would bring their pillows from home. *or* Each of the clerks decided he/she would bring a pillow from home.

---

[6] See, for instance, a thorough discussion of both the historical justifications for using the masculine pronoun as "pseudogeneric" and a summary of psychological studies about its impact, in DEBORA SCHEIKART, "The Gender Neutral Pronoun Redefined," 20 WOMEN'S RIGHTS L. REPORTER, 1.

2. **Drop the pronoun** where possible:

 On the first day, the average summer associate asks his supervising partner ten questions about format and office policy.

On the first day, the average summer associate asks the supervising partner ten questions about format and office policy.

3. Refer to people by **occupation or qualification** instead of gender.

 Improvement in water quality in major cities is man's goal for the next decade.

The voters' goal for the next decade is improvement in water quality in major cities.

 The policeman asked for two weeks off to attend a Zen conference.

The police officer asked for two weeks off to attend a Zen conference.

4. **Vary** the document's pronouns from "he" to "she"—if and only if the variation does not change the meaning of your document and does not result in utter silliness.

 Many practicing attorneys dream of becoming law professors. One attorney may envision leaving his 60-hour week behind. She may look forward to the intellectual stimulation of her imagined students.

Try These

What would you do about word choice in the following situations? See answers, page 113.

1. You are returning a business letter to a banker, who has signed an initial inquiry as "J.W. Smith." What is a proper salutation?

2. Preparing a group-mailing tax-advice letter to a group of sculptors, you need to refer to the artist who has traveling exhibitions, to the artist who uses a publicist, etc. How do you avoid the "he" or "she" pronoun?

3. You have spent several months researching a question for a client, an ardent feminist. Throughout the final memorandum of explanation, you have consistently used "he" as a generic reference to "anyone under the law who . . .". Now what?

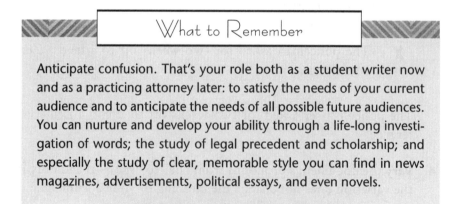

What to Remember

Anticipate confusion. That's your role both as a student writer now and as a practicing attorney later: to satisfy the needs of your current audience and to anticipate the needs of all possible future audiences. You can nurture and develop your ability through a life-long investigation of words; the study of legal precedent and scholarship; and especially the study of clear, memorable style you can find in news magazines, advertisements, political essays, and even novels.

CONCLUDING EXERCISES

Correct the examples in this concluding quiz that mixes the word problems you've just reviewed. Look for jargon, wordiness, pronoun antecedents, noun strings, nominalizations, treacherous words, and unnecessary gender-based nouns and pronouns. See possible answers, page 113.

1. The associate took many late night excursions into her boss' break room.

2. When the associate saw the secretary in the office after 10 p.m., she was worried that she took her job too seriously.

3. Whilst she approached her job seriously, the firm's unequivocal view was that excess and unnecessary time distinguishable on a time sheet would be exorcized post haste.

4. As a matter of fact, there was extra time throughout her last time sheet that was held to be inappropriate.

5. The senior partner asked her to please make a statement of why she was interposing an objection to the edit of her time sheets.

Circle the correct word.

6. The new associate's assignment was composed of / comprised of three international water issues.

7. She was asked to be discrete / discreet about the sensitive ramifications.

8. The associate lay / laid the first draft beside the coffee pot in her break room.

9. One of the secretaries was able to imply / infer from the draft's heading that the associate was involved in the case.

10. The secretary knew its / it's worth outside the office setting.

An attorney worried all morning over the awkward options for beginning a letter he had written to one female and four male bankers. Rather than the bulky and formal "Dear Sirs and Madam," his solution was to drop the woman's name from the inside address list, address the letter in the shorter "Dear Sirs," and to add, at the bottom of the letter, "c.c. Texanna McPhail."

Punctuation has long been considered the stronghold of inflexible and prescriptive rules. This tradition is unfortunate. To a great degree, punctuation is variable, flexible, and even imaginative.

WILLIAM D. DRAKE, THE WAY TO PUNCTUATE, xii (1971)

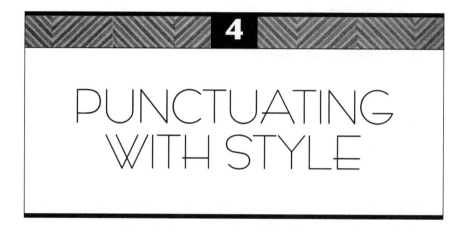

4

PUNCTUATING WITH STYLE

This is your last look at your draft: This time, return to that organized, polished document you're creating, and review the punctuation that holds it together, separates portions of it, and sets its pace and meaning.

Overview

+ Punctuating sentences
+ Punctuating words

When early writers added punctuation to their written speeches in the third century B.C., they signaled places for speakers to pause. The different marks signaled the reader/speaker's pause length. Today's punctuation is governed by only a few rules for those signals.

PUNCTUATING SENTENCES

1. Complete sentence.

The initial drafters of the 1983 Rules of Professional Responsibility considered the language of the old dishonesty rule to be unduly broad.

2. Sentence, *conjunction* sentence.

> *, and*
> *, or*
> *, nor*
> *, but*
> *, yet*

The comma is not always essential in all types of writing, but legal writers signal an impending new subject/verb with it.

3. Complete sentence; complete sentence.

Rules such as Canon 22 were hortatory; they were "intended for edification rather than for enforcement."

4. Complete sentence; *conjunctive adverb*, complete sentence.

> *; therefore,*
> *; however,*
> *; nevertheless,*
> *; consequently,*
> *; furthermore,*

Rules such as Canon 22 were hortatory; *indeed,* they were "intended for edification rather than for enforcement."

5. Complete , *interruptor,* sentence.
      , on the other hand,
      , for example,
      , in fact,

The predecessor to Rule 8.4(c), *for example*, has been construed to require a lawyer to reveal the existence of a Mary Carter Agreement.

6. Complete , *citation,* sentence.

In the recent case of *In re Gatti*, 8 P.3d 969 (Or. 2000), the Oregon Supreme Court sanctioned a lawyer who misrepresented his identity while attempting to investigate a claim of insurance fraud.

7. *Adverb* incomplete sentence, complete sentence.

Although
After
Because
While
When

Although the court acknowledged that some misrepresentations are essential if an attorney is to successfully investigate violations of the law, it refused to recognize any exceptions for lawyers who engage in dishonesty.

8. Complete sentence *adverb* incomplete sentence.

although
after
because
while
when

The court refused to recognize an exception for lawyers who engage in dishonesty *although* it had acknowledged that some misrepresentations are essential if an attorney is to successfully investigate violations of law.

9. *Short introductory phrase*, complete sentence. (optional comma)

By July 1990 he had turned in his resignation.
By July 1990, he had turned in his resignation.

10. Sentence ending with a *colon*: dramatic saying, second sentence that explains the first, separated list, list that completes sentence.

Dramatic saying: Ghandi admitted to authorities that he knew a lot about prisons: African and Indian.

Second sentence explains: In one sense, this Student Note accomplishes nothing new: the benefits and dangers inherent in judicial discretion are well known.

Separated list: If writers choose to create a list that follows a complete sentence but is **not** a part of the textual sentence's grammar, then they should follow the following seven conventions:

1. Colon introduction.
2. Indentation.
3. Grammatical parallel.
4. Capital letters.
5. Numbered items.
6. Periods at the end of each item.
7. No "or" or "and" for culmination.

List completing sentence: When a list is a grammatical part of the sentence, the items to be enumerated must belong to the same class, with a common idea introduced before the colon. Then, for lists within a formal text, writers can choose to set the list apart from the text:

1. by introducing the list with a colon;
2. by indenting all of each item and numbering each item;
3. by beginning each item with a lower-case letter;
4. by concluding each item but the last with a semicolon;
5. by placing a semicolon and "and" or "or" after the next-to-last item; and
6. by concluding the item with a period unless the list does not conclude the textual sentence.

Do not use a colon between a verb and its object or complement, or between a preposition and its object.

 A prisoner has: no privacy of mail and little access to medical treatment.

 The law firm requested his resume consist of: educational background, work experience, and references.

Capitalization after a colon is optional, but most writers capitalize complete sentences after the colon and leave fragments in lower case:

We must all accept a priority: Your priority was never on my list.

11. *Commas and periods,* like "these," go inside quotation marks.

First, the Canon, on its face, limited the duty of candor to "conduct of the lawyer before the Court and the other lawyers."

12. *Colons and semicolons* go "outside"; this rule is an American rule.

First, the 1908 ABA Canon 22 limited the duty of candor to "conduct of the lawyer before the Court and the other lawyers"; second, the Canon was confined to specific types of litigation and negotiation conduct.

13. *A quotation* over 49 words is indented and single-spaced. According to legal editors, [1]

> If the quotation is longer than 49 words (or if you have a special reason for setting quoted material outside your main text), signal the indented quotation with single-spaced indented format but do *not* use quotation marks: the formatting signals the direct quotation. If the quotation is not a part of your textual sentence, lead into it with a colon. If the quotation picks up your textual syntax, do not add any punctuation before indenting and single spacing.

14. *Items in a series* require commas between items and before the "and" or "or."

He was accused of breaking and entering, assault and battery, and rape.

15. A list that contains a *comma within a list* of items requires *semicolons* between the items listed.

The dishonesty rule creates an incentive for lawyers to refrain from conduct that might otherwise be advantageous to their clients by increasing the risk of disciplinary action, such as the one under investigation; by financial loss; and by the attendant social stigma that attaches to a lawyer accused of an ethical violation.

16. *Dates* containing both day and year require *two commas*.

He is to appear in court July 15, 2004, unless the state bar exonerates him.

He is to appear in court July 2004 unless the state bar exonerates him.

---

[1] The Association of Legal Writing Directors & Darby Dickerson, ALWD Citation Manual: A Professional System of Citation (2d ed., Aspen 2003), Rule 48.5(a); The Bluebook: A Uniform System of Citation, Rule 5.1 (16th ed. 1996).

PUNCTUATING WORDS

17. *Ellipses and spacing* indicate that you have omitted material from a passage being quoted. (A legal ellipsis mark is composed of *three spaced* periods.)[2]

There is no subjective good faith excuse for attorney negligence:

> A lawyer in Texas is held to the standard of care which would be exercised by a reasonably prudent attorney. . . . [Jury should evaluate] based on the information the attorney has at the time of the alleged act of negligence. In some instances an attorney is required to make tactical or strategic decisions. Ostensibly, the good faith exception was created to protect this unique attorney work product. However, allowing the attorney to assert his subjective good faith . . . creates too great a burden for wronged clients to overcome.

Cosgrove v. Grimes, 772 S.W.2d 662.

18. *Brackets* signal change in quoted material:[3]

(a) missing words or letters;

(b) capitals changed to lower case and lower-cased words changed to capitals to fit the sense of the quotation into your text;

(c) additions that help explain ambiguous material in a quotation;

---

[2] The Association of Legal Writing Directors & Darby Dickerson, ALWD Citation Manual: A Professional System of Citation (2d ed., Aspen 2003), Rule 50.3(b); The Bluebook: A Uniform System of Citation, Rule 5.3(b)(ii) (16th ed. 1996). When you omit material after a period within the original text, add a fourth dot as the final punctuation. If you omit material before the sentence ends, follow it with white space before the first dot. You should have a complete sentence on both sides of the four-dot ellipsis. Legal writers do not use ellipsis points before a block quotation beginning with a complete sentence even though they have (usually) left out material from the original.

[3] The Association of Legal Writing Directors & Darby Dickerson, ALWD Citation Manual: A Professional System of Citation (2d ed., Aspen 2003), Rule 49.2; The Bluebook: A Uniform System of Citation, Rule 5.2 (16th ed. 1996).

(d) your own comments inserted into quoted material; and

(e) the word "sic" to indicate an error repeated from the original ("sic" is a complete word meaning "in this manner" or "thus").

Following are examples of correctly placed brackets:

Mark Wojcik suggested, "The book [*Introduction to Legal English*] can and should be supplemented with additional materials."

The contract specifically provides that "$10,000 shall be paid to the surrogate [appellant] upon entry of the judgment fully terminating parental rights of the surrogate." <u>See</u> Surrogate Mother Contract Agreement 4.

"[P]risoner petitions . . . are the first line of defense against unconstitutional violations." <u>Bounds v. Smith</u>, 430 U.S. 817, 827, 97 S. Ct. 1491, 1498 (1977).

19. Two adjectives before a noun, or a string of nouns before the main noun, are combined with a *hyphen*:

State-appointed negotiators offered a week of free training to help the courts.

(*See* Chapter 3.) Remember, however, that adverbs ending in -ly should not be hyphenated.

20. *Dashes* signal a break in thought and writing.

The court has one consistent goal—to provide justice for the people of this state.

Dashes differ from hyphens in both typography and purpose. Dashes are typed with two hyphens and no spaces on either side. Dashes *separate*; hyphens *draw together*.

21. *Apostrophes* signal possessives, not plurals.

Students' notebooks (more than one student and notebook) are sold at the Co-op.

A student's notebook (one student, one notebook) costs $3.95.

English pronouns have their own possessive case (his, my, their, our) and **do not** require an apostrophe.

 The company determined it's future with a quick vote.

Nouns, including numbers and letters, do not use apostrophes to create plurals.

 The Miller's were visiting their daughter when the car crashed through the wall.

All winners of the 100s were given a one-hundred dollar bill.

The 60s were a period of protest and freedom.

The professor awarded only three TAs a job offer.

What to Remember

As boring as punctuation rules seem, they nevertheless perform an important role in communicating. English doesn't have so many punctuation rules that they overwhelm writers: so learn the few rules; study the options; then allow yourself some play—readers will appreciate it and see your educated variances as a sign of intelligence and sophistication.

CONCLUDING EXERCISES

Correct these concluding quizzes that mix the punctuation rules you have just reviewed. See answers, page 114.

1. If confidence sinks too low members of the public will cease looking to the legal system for resolution to problems.

2. A court must weigh the dangers of vagueness and discriminatory enforcement against the need to protect the integrity of the judicial system, the goal of protecting the interests of the client, which is admittedly paternalistic, and the need to encourage honesty among lawyers, which maintains the integrity of the profession.

3. Some opinions have held that Rule 8.4(c) requires a lawyer to bring possible mistakes to the attention of opposing counsel and others have held that a violation may occur through the acts or omissions of a third party.

4. It seeks first to avoid the need to abandon Rule 8.4(c) by proposing a framework for the analysis of future cases arising under the rule, second it attempts to focus attention to the dangers inherent in broad grants of judicial discretion.

5. A court must weigh the dangers of vagueness and discriminatory enforcement against the following—the need to protect the integrity of the judicial system, the goal of protecting the interests of clients, and the need to encourage honesty among lawyers.

6. When examining a statute, a court must ask whether the statute either:

   . . . fails to give a person of ordinary intelligence fair notice that his contemplated conduct is forbidden by the statute, or is so indefinite that it encourages arbitrary and erratic arrests and convictions.

7. The rule creates an incentive on the part of a lawyer to avoid overly aggressive conduct which might be construed as a violation.

8. Canon 22 of the 1908 Canons imposed upon lawyers a general duty of "candor and fairness".

9. Where an act of dishonesty has not injured a client or someone to whom the lawyer owes a fiduciary duty, then at least one goal of discipline is not compromised the goal of protecting clients.

10. Given the problems with attorneys' ethics, some might argue that all law school courses should include discussions of ethical issues; specific issues with concrete examples.

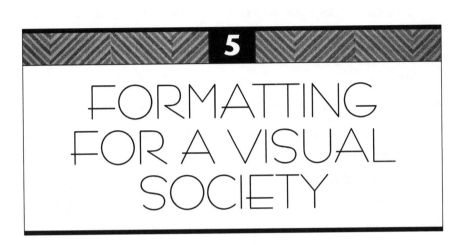

FORMATTING FOR A VISUAL SOCIETY

Remember the advice in the *Message to Students*: Your readers are not going to look at your document because they have extra time or because they need entertainment. Rather, they need information—and fast. To help them find that information, writers should make each document as attractive and accessible as possible. You are already the victim of the subliminal seduction of law schools: all opinions look like each other, and all sample memoranda look like other sample memoranda. You need to remember your own dismay at your first sight of these documents and break the pattern.

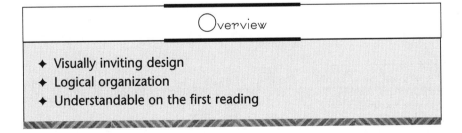

Overview

✦ Visually inviting design
✦ Logical organization
✦ Understandable on the first reading

S O L U T I O N S

1. Add **white space** throughout the document with margin, spaces between paragraphs, space around tabulation, and graphics.

2. Create an **initial road map** that contains both the conclusion and brief road map of what will follow.

3. Adjust **paragraphs' lengths** so that they are not all the same (long) length.

4. Include **side bars** for summaries or headings for client documents.

5. Include **graphics** where possible and label them so readers can skim the accompanying text.

6. Avoid **ALL CAPITAL LETTERS** where possible (don't change trademark names, or the capital/strikeout system of some legislation).

7. Use **bold face type** for emphasis, where applicable.

8. Use an **appendix** for explanatory material.

9. Study **proximity, alignment, repetition, and contrast**, and apply these techniques where possible.[1]

---

[1] ROBIN WILLIAMS, THE NON-DESIGNER'S DESIGN BOOK (Peachtree Press, 1994). Thanks to Ruth Anne Robbins, Rutgers School of Law—Camden, for re-acquainting me with this valuable resource.

What to Remember

Lawyers write to the public as well as to other lawyers. When you are ready to produce any document, see it as your audience will see it and present your major points up front, perhaps even boldly. No one suggests you create new forms for court filings; still, no federal rule requires lawyers to bore their daily readers with massive pages of repetitive black ink, either. Using white space, side bars, and a variety of fonts can both enliven and inform the very people you hope will read your entire document.

Example 1A. A sample student memorandum

QUESTION PRESENTED: Does an attorney commit malpractice when he cites a case that has been overturned and this results in an adverse decision in litigation?

CONCLUSION: Yes. An attorney who cites to an overturned case does not act as a reasonably prudent attorney. If the failure results in harm to the client, the attorney is negligent and thus has committed malpractice.

FACTS: Our client, Lima, Inc., an importer of limes, was represented by John Gerardi in a litigation matter. In his brief, Gerardi relied heavily on a case that, unknown to him, the Texas Supreme Court had overturned six months before Lima's scheduled hearing.

. . . .

good road map but
not highlighted

DISCUSSION: Lima's malpractice claim against Gerardi hinges on the legal issue of negligence, particularly the extent of Gerardi's duty to research the law properly and the breach of this duty. In Texas, a malpractice claim is based on the law of negligence. Cosgrove v. Grimes, 774 S.W.2d 662, 664 (Tex. 1989). To show that Gerardi was negligent, Lima must show that Gerardi had a duty to Lima, that he breached it, and that this breach was the proximate cause of Lima's harm. Cosgrove, 774 S.W.2d at 665. An attorney has a duty to properly research the law, and breaches this duty when he fails to do so. Morrill v. Graham, 27 Tex. 646, 651 (1864); Walder v. Texas, 85 S.W.3d 824, 827 (Ct. App.—Waco 2002).

. . . .

no headings

When a lawyer undertakes a matter on behalf of a client, the lawyer must exercise ordinary care and diligence in handling the client's matter, including using the skills normally possessed by competent lawyers. Savings Bank v. Ward, 100 U.S. 195, 199 (1879). The lawyer breaches his duty to his client when he fails to meet this standard. Savings Bank, 100 U.S. at 199.

. . . .

no visual cues to
help reader
anticipate
organization

Checking cases to see whether they are still reliable precedent is a central part of a lawyer's responsibility. The Texas rules of professional responsibility require a lawyer to be able to undertake "the analysis of precedent" to be considered competent. Texas Disciplinary R. Prof'l Conduct, 1.01, Cmt. 3 (2002).

. . . .

Because Gerardi had a duty and breached it, and because that breach was the proximate cause of injury, all of the elements of negligence are present. Thus, Lima may sustain a malpractice action against Gerardi.

Example 1B. Student memorandum with headings, white space, and initial road map

QUESTION PRESENTED: Does an attorney commit malpractice when he cites a case that has been overturned and this results in an adverse decision in litigation?

alignment—all major headings are flush left, bold

CONCLUSION: Yes. An attorney who cites to an overturned case does not act as a reasonably prudent attorney. If the failure results in harm to the client, the attorney is negligent and thus has committed malpractice.

conclusion up front

FACTS: Our client, Lima, Inc., an importer of limes, was represented by John Gerardi in a litigation matter. In his brief, Gerardi relied heavily on a case that, unknown to him, the Texas Supreme Court had overturned six months before Lima's scheduled hearing. Lima lost the case and was forced to pay $250,000 in damages. The court explicitly made its decision based on Gerardi's reliance on the overturned decision and admonished Gerardi for his failure to Shepardize. Lima has engaged us to sue Gerardi for malpractice.

DISCUSSION: Lima's malpractice claim against Gerardi hinges on the legal issue of negligence, particularly the extent of Gerardi's duty to research the law properly and the breach of this duty. In Texas, a malpractice claim is based on the law of negligence. Cosgrove v. Grimes, 774 S.W.2d 662, 664 (Tex. 1989). To show that Gerardi was negligent, Lima must show
    1) that Gerardi had a duty to Lima, that he breached it, and
    2) that this breach was the proximate cause of Lima's harm. Cosgrove, 774 S.W.2d at 665. An attorney has a duty to properly research the law, and breaches this duty when he fails to do so. Morrill v. Graham, 27 Tex. 646, 651 (1864); Walder v. Texas, 85 S.W.3d 824, 827 (Ct. App.—Waco 2002). Failure to check legal precedents is a breach of this duty. Two Thirty Nine Joint Venture v. Joe, 60 S.W.3d 896, 905 (Tex. App. Dallas 2001—pet. granted); Texas Disciplinary R. Prof'l Conduct, 1.01. Cmt. 3 (2002). Where the breach proximately causes harm to the client, the attorney will be liable for malpractice. Two Thirty Nine Joint Venture, 60 S.W.3d at 896.

*legal issue (negligence) as first sentence, followed by set-up with indented, **aligned** numbers and bold-faced numbers*

1. Duty and Breach
An attorney has a duty to properly research the law and breaches this duty when he fails to do so. When a lawyer undertakes a matter on behalf of a client, the lawyer must exercise ordinary care and diligence in handling the client's matter, including using the skills normally possessed by competent lawyers. Savings Bank v. Ward, 100 U.S. 195, 199 (1879). The lawyer breaches his duty to his client when . . .

headings follow set-up

*repetition of indented left major headings, **contrasting** bold face*

. . . .

Conclusion
Because Gerardi had a duty and breached it, and because that breach was the proximate cause of injury, all of the elements of negligence are present. Thus, Lima may sustain a malpractice action against Gerardi.

repetition of set-up and legal question

Example 2A. Client letter emphasizing content only

GETMAN & SELCOV, LLP   ATTORNEYS AT LAW

52 S. Manheim Blvd., 2ⁿᵈ Floor   (914) 255-9370
New Paltz, NY 12561   fax (914) 255-3629

Julius Getman (DC bar only), of counsel   Richard B. Wolf (NY and DC), of counsel

VIA FEDERAL EXPRESS   April 5, 2004

Professor David Sokolow
University of Texas Law School
727 E. 26th Street
Austin, Texas 78702

Dear Professor Sokolow:

Please find enclosed a Subpoena Duces Tecum Without Deposition which has been issued by the U.S. District Court, Middle District of Florida, Jacksonville Division, Case No. 99-978-Civ-J-11D, for any and all documents regarding Lillian Lander (DOB: 9/16/46; SSN: 458-48-3195). We would appreciate your providing any and all items in the attached subpoena. These documents should include a complete statement of all opinions expressed and the basis and reasons therefor; the data or other information considered in forming the opinion(s); any exhibits to be used as a summary of or support for the opinion(s); expert qualifications, including a list of all publications authored within the preceding ten years (include your resume); compensation amount(s); and a list of cases in which you have testified as an expert at trial or by deposition within the preceding four years.

Please submit your statement for reproduction charges, and we will reimburse you that same amount. Thank you for your assistance in this matter. Please do not hesitate to call if you require further information.

Yours truly,

Susan Sharlot
Legal Assistant

Margin annotations:

no identifying information

dense information block with no hierarchy

reader skimming quickly would assume all writer needs is invoice

Example 2B. Revised client letter: white space, tabulation, contrast

GETMAN & SELCOV, LLP   ATTORNEYS AT LAW

52 S. Manheim Blvd., 2nd Floor   (914) 255-9370
New Paltz, NY 12561   fax (914) 255-3629

Julius Getman (DC bar only), of counsel   Richard B. Wolf (NY and DC), of counsel

VIA FEDERAL EXPRESS   April 5, 2004
Professor David Sokolow
University of Texas Law School
727 E. 26th Street
Austin, Texas 78702

RE: Lillian Lander vs. Al Kayda

Case No. 99-978-Civ-J-11D   *bold* **contrast**
provides context

Dear Professor Sokolow:

We are asking that you comply with the Subpoena Duces Tecum Without   active, up-front
Deposition in this case. The U.S. District Court, Middle District of   request
Florida, Jacksonville Division, asks for any and all documents regarding
Lillian Lander (DOB: 9/16/46; SSN: 458-48-3195). Please provide any
items in the attached subpoena, including:

1. **opinions** expressed and the basis of their reasoning;   **alignment,**
2. **data or other information** considered in forming the opinion(s);   **proximity** of
3. **exhibits** to be used as a summary of or support for the opinion(s);   items, and
4. **expert qualifications,** including a list of all publications authored   **repetition** of bold
within the preceding ten years (include your resume);   face
5. **compensation** amount(s); and a
6. **list of cases** in which you have testified as an expert at trial or by deposition within the preceding four years.

As you will see, the **deadline** for this information is **May 5, 2004.**   subtle, larger type
with bold face
contrasts and
If you will submit your statement for reproduction charges, we will re-   emphasizes
imburse you that same amount. Thank you for assisting us. Please do not   deadline
hesitate to call me if you require further information.

Yours truly,

Susan Sharlot
Legal Assistant

Example 3A. Law student resume

JACKIE CARTON
909 E. 49th Street
Bloomington, Indiana 47408

home: 812-333-1395   work: 812-333-1515
Qualifications

no contrasts

College graduate, first-year law student; flexible, inquisitive; motivated to learn and grow in responsibility and skills; dependable; competent legal research and writing, typing skills; and excellent telephone and people skills.

no proximity of headings to information

Skills and Experiences

alignment provides no hierarchy

Organizing—section 1 ambassador to law student council; recruited students into university as Student Ambassador; Teaching Assistant; mentored students; founded International Affairs Club; gathered volunteers, investigated hotel space, transportation, convention rooms for American Freedom Network

Office experience—data entry (membership, donations, shipping orders), answered telephone, delivered messages; Employee Award two months

People skills—bilingual, Spanish; established campus-wide club with variety of majors and backgrounds; Student Ambassador College of Arts

repetition of alignment

Work Experience

Spring 2001	Office help	Kinkos
Fall, spring 2002	Teaching Assistant	Political Science
Summer 2000	Enumerator	Federal Bureau of Census
Spring 2000	Fiscal Intern	Indiana Legislature
Summer 1999	Ranch hand, horse trainer	Elsewhere Farms

Education and Training

inverted order

B.A. with Honors, Indiana University, International Affairs 2002
Indianapolis Community College, 6 hrs (3.4), 1998
Language Arts Academy, Johns High School, Anderson, Indiana, graduated 1998

Example 3B. Law student resume

Jackie Carton
909 E. 49th Street
Bloomington, Indiana 47408

home: 812-333-1395/work: 333-1515
jcarton@iu.edu

strong, contrasting
type for main
categories

Qualifications

strong left
alignment

▲ Legal research and writing skills, computer skills
▲ Legislative, fiscal experience
▲ Bilingual (Spanish) public speaker, organizer

second left
alignment for
subsections

Education

g.p.a. slightly
larger font,
centered

▲ B.A. Indiana University, with Honors, International Affairs 2002,
G.P.A. 3.8
▲ Indianapolis Community College, 6 hrs (3.4), 1998
▲ Language Arts Academy, Johns High School, Anderson, IN graduated 1998

Work Experience

all subheads
aligned and
symbol **repeated**

▲ Teaching Assistant	2002	Indiana University Dept. of Political Science
▲ Fiscal Intern	2000	Indiana legislature
▲ Enumerator	2000	Federal Bureau of Census
▲ Customer relations	2001	Kinkos

Skills and Experiences

repeated
alignment

▲ Organizing:	Section 1 Ambassador to law school Student Council
	Indiana University Student Ambassador
	Established campus-wide International Affairs Club
	Scheduled speaking and promotion events
	Investigated space, transportation, convention rooms
▲ Office experience:	Data entry, American Freedom Network
	Solicited membership and contributions
	Employee Award two months, Kinkos
▲ People skills:	Taught freshman political science, Indiana University
	Encouraged contributors, American Freedom Network

References

eye-catching bold
lines repeated

▲ Prof. Michael Tigger, Indiana University School of Law,
812-333-7878
▲ Dean Francis Hoole, Indiana University, 812-333-9882

91

Example 4A. Law student cover letter

Fredrick Youngdale, III
111 Greenberg Drive
Youngdale, Florida 33315
954-874-4598
fyoungd@aol.com

September 16, 2005

Mrs. Hazel Moore
Hiring Partner
Bracewell & Patterson
1100 Pennzoil Place
Houston, Texas

no initial information

Dear Mrs. Moore,

weak introduction

Your firm uses second-year law students during the summer. I am apply-ing for that position. I would like to visit your office for an interview when I will be in Houston, Nov. 16-19. Please let me know which day and what time would fit into your busy schedule. I am currently a second-year law student at the University of FarWest Florida. Still, Texas calls. I am currently taking Trial Advocacy and will participate in a mock trial later this fall. As you can tell, I am interested in trial work. Does your firm offer trial experience to summer clerks? These and other questions I hope to have answered in our interview in November. Last summer I worked at my father's firm for six weeks, Youngdale & Youngdale of Miami. I drafted documents and assisted the younger asso-ciates as they prepared for big trials. As you can see, I have some legal experience and am eager for more.

one solid information block

buried skills, experiences

Sincerely,

Fredrick Youngdale, III

Example 4B. Law student cover letter

Fredrick Youngdale, III
111 Greenberg Drive
Youngdale, Florida 33315
954-874-4598
fyoungd@aol.com

September 16, 2005

Mrs. Hazel Moore
Hiring Partner
Bracewell & Patterson
1100 Pennzoil Place
Houston, Texas

Re: summer internship

Dear Mrs. Moore,

Your August advertisement in *Florida Lawyer* caught my interest. Fred Ledbetter, a second-year associate at Bracewell & Patterson in Dallas, recommended that I contact you because your firm focuses on trial work. As a second-year student at FarWest Florida School of Law, I have a strong, demonstrated interest in trial work, as evidenced by my participation this fall in an elective moot court. I would welcome the opportunity to work for your firm as a summer clerk.

In the course of researching Bracewell & Patterson, I discovered that your firm frequently represents clients who are involved in disputes with the DEA and INS over the seizure of their boats.

- I grew up around boats.
- Last summer I worked on admiralty questions at Youngdale & Youngdale as a summer associate.
- This year I am enrolled in Admiralty Law.
- I plan to focus on Admiralty Law when I graduate.

I would like to visit your office for an interview when I will be in Houston, Nov. 16-19. I hope to meet with you or someone in your office. I will contact you within the next two weeks and, if possible, arrange a time to meet that would be convenient. If you prefer, you can contact me at the number or email address above. Thank you for your consideration.

Sincerely,

Fredrick Youngdale, III

Enclosure
Cc: Jack Gershwin, Recruiting Coordinator

Margin annotations:

up-front statement of purpose

introduction acknowledges where applicant learned of job opening

reference to specific interest

shows specific interest in firm— not merely a form letter

here, **alignment** of skills and experience; **repetition** of bullet dots; **contrast** of list to body of text; followed by white space

short paragraphs

has researched firm's personnel

Example 5A. 1965 D.C. Court of Appeals opinion

Ora Lee WILLIAMS, Appellant
v.
WALKER-THOMAS FURNITURE COMPANY, Appellee,
William THORNE et al., Appellants,
v.
WALKER-THOMAS FURNITURE COMPANY, Appellee.
Nos. 18604, 18605.

United States Court of Appeals
District of Columbia Circuit.
Argued April 9, 1965.
Decided Aug. 11, 1965.

J. SKELLY WRIGHT, Circuit Judge:

Appellee, Walker-Thomas Furniture Company, operates a retail furniture store in the District of Columbia. During the period from 1957 to 1962 each appellant in these cases purchased a number of household items from Walker-Thomas, for which payment was to be made in installments. The terms of each purchase were contained in a printed form contract which set forth the value of the purchased item and purported to lease the item to appellant for a stipulated monthly rent payment. The contract then provided, in substance, that title would remain in Walker-Thomas until the total of all the monthly payments made equaled the stated value of the item, at which time appellants could take title. In the event of a default in the payment of any monthly installment, Walker-Thomas could repossess the item.

The contract further provided that "the amount of each periodical installment payment to be made by [purchaser] to the Company under this present lease shall be inclusive of and not in addition to the amount of each installment payment to be made by [purchaser] under such prior leases, bills or accounts; *and all payments now and hereafter made by [purchaser] shall be credited pro rata on all outstanding leases, bills and accounts* due the Company by [purchaser] at the time each such payment is made." (Emphasis added.) The effect of this rather obscure provision was to keep a balance due on every item purchased until the balance due on all items, whenever purchased, was liquidated. As a result, the debt incurred at the time of purchase of each item was secured by the right to repossess all the items previously purchased by the same purchaser, and each new item purchased automatically became subject to a security interest arising out of the previous dealings.

On May 12, 1962, appellant Thorne purchased an item described as a Daveno, three tables, and two lamps, having total stated value of $391.10. Shortly thereafter, he defaulted on his monthly payments and appellee sought to replevy all the items purchased since the first transaction in 1958. Similarly, on April 17, 1962, appellant Williams bought a stereo set of stated value of $514.95. She too defaulted shortly thereafter, and appellee sought to replevy all the items purchased since December, 1957. The Court of General Sessions granted judgment for appellee. The District of Columbia Court of Appeals affirmed, and we granted appellants' motion for leave to appeal to this court.

Appellants' principal contention, rejected by both the trial and the appellate courts below, is that these contracts, or at least some of them, are unconscionable and, hence, not enforceable. In its opinion in Williams v. Walker-Thomas Furniture Company, 198 A.2d 914, 916 (1964), the District of Columbia Court of Appeals explained its rejection of this contention as follows:

"Appellants' second argument presents a more serious question. The record reveals that prior to the last purchase appellant had reduced the balance in her account to $164. The last purchase, a stereo set, raised the balance due to $678. Significantly, at the time of this and the preceding purchases, appellee was aware of appellant's financial position. The reverse side of the stereo contract listed the name of appellant's social worker and her $218 monthly stipend from the government. Nevertheless, with full knowledge that appellant had to feed, clothe and support both herself and seven children on this amount, appellee sold her a $514 stereo set.

"We cannot condemn too strongly appellee's conduct. It raises serious questions of sharp practice and irresponsible business dealings. A review of the legislation in the District of Columbia affecting retail sales and the pertinent decisions of the highest court in this jurisdiction disclose, however, no ground upon which this court can declare the contracts in question contrary to public policy. We note that were the Maryland Retail Installment Sales Act, Art. 83 128–153, or its equivalent, in force in the District of Columbia, we could grant appellant appropriate relief. We think Congress should consider corrective legislation to protect the public from such exploitive contracts as were utilized in the case at bar."

We do not agree that the court lacked the power to refuse enforcement to contracts found to be unconscionable. In other jurisdictions, it has been held as a matter of common law that unconscionable contracts are not enforceable.

[1, 2] Congress has recently enacted the Uniform Commercial Code, which specifically provides that the court may refuse to enforce a contract which it finds to be unconscionable at the time it was made.

. . . .

[3–10] Unconscionability has generally been recognized to include an absence of meaningful choice on the part of one of the parties together with contract terms which are unreasonably favorable to the other party. Whether a meaningful choice is present in a particular case can only be determined by consideration of all the circumstances surrounding the transaction. In many cases the meaningfulness of the choice is negated by a gross inequality of bargaining power.

. . . .

[11–13] In determining reasonableness or fairness, the primary concern must be with the terms of the contract considered in light of the circumstances existing when the contract was made.

. . . .

[14] Because the trial court and the appellate court did not feel that enforcement could be refused, no findings were made on the possible unconscionability of the contracts in these cases. Since the record is not sufficient for our deciding the issue as a matter of law, the cases must be remanded to the trial court for further proceedings.

So ordered.

Example 5B. Revised opinion

Ora Lee WILLIAMS, Appellant,
v.
WALKER-THOMAS FURNITURE COMPANY, Appellee.
William THORNE et al., Appellants,
v.
WALKER-THOMAS FURNITURE COMPANY, Appellee.
Nos. 18604, 18605

United States Court of Appeals
District of Columbia Circuit
Argued April 9, 1965.
Decided Aug. 11, 1964.

Background: Appellants signed a series of contracts for furniture. The balance due on every item purchased continued until the total debt for all items was liquidated. The Court of General Sessions found no common law ground by which they could declare the contracts were contrary to public policy and thus found for the furniture company. The District of Columbia Court of Appeals agreed and affirmed that decision.

Holding: This court, however, holds that where a contract is unconscionable due to the term and circumstances of the contract, that contract is unenforceable in a court of law. We therefore reverse the decisions below and remand the cases to the trial court to determine if these circumstances and terms were so unfair and unreasonable that they were unconscionable as a matter of law.

Procedural background and facts of contracts:
J. SKELLY WRIGHT, Circuit Judge:
 Appellee, Walker-Thomas Furniture Company, operates a retail furniture store in the District of Columbia. During the period from 1957 to 1962 each appellant in these cases purchased a number of household items from Walker-Thomas, for which payment was to be made in installments. The terms of each purchase were contained in a printed form contract which set forth the value of the purchased item and purported to lease the item to appellant for a stipulated monthly rent payment. The contract then provided, in substance, that title would remain in Walker-Thomas until the total of all the monthly payments made equaled the stated value of the item, at which time appellants could take title. In the event of a default in the payment of any monthly installment, Walker-Thomas could repossess the item.
 On May 12, 1962, appellant Thorne purchased an item described as a Daveno, three tables, and two lamps, having total stated value of $391.10. Shortly thereafter, he defaulted on his monthly payments and appellee sought to replevy all the items purchased since the first transaction in 1958. Similarly, on April 17, 1962, appellant Williams bought a stereo set of stated value of $514.95. She too defaulted shortly thereafter, and appellee sought to replevy all the items purchased since December, 1957.

Arguments:
 Appellants' principal contention, rejected by both the trial and the appellate courts below, is that these contracts, or at least some of them, are unconscionable and, hence, not enforceable. In its opinion in Williams v. Walker-Thomas Furniture Company, 198 A.2d 914, 916 (1964), the District of Columbia Court of Appeals explained its rejection of this contention as follows:
 "Appellants' second argument presents a more serious question. The record reveals that prior to the last purchase appellant had reduced the balance in her account to $164. The last purchase, a stereo set, raised the balance due to $678. Significantly, at the time of this and the preceding purchases, appellee was aware of appellant's financial position. The reverse side of the stereo contract listed the name of appellant's social worker and her $218 monthly stipend from the government. Nevertheless, with full knowledge that appellant had to feed, clothe and support both herself and seven children on this amount, appellee sold her a $514 stereo set. . . ."

Discussion:
A. The Court has the power to refuse enforcement of unconscionable contracts.
 We do not agree that the court lacked the power to refuse enforcement to contracts found to be unconscionable. In other jurisdictions, it has been held as a matter of common law that unconscionable contracts are not enforceable.

. . . .

B. U.C.C. codification of the common law rule of unconscionability is persuasive authority.
 Congress has recently enacted the Uniform Commercial Code, which specifically provides that the court may refuse to enforce a contract which it finds to be unconscionable at the time it was made.

. . . .

 1. Circumstances
 Whether a meaningful choice is present in a particular case can only be determined by consideration of all the circumstances surrounding the transaction. In many cases the meaningfulness of the choice is negated by a gross inequality of bargaining power.

. . . .

 2. Reasonableness or fairness
 In determining reasonableness or fairness, the primary concern must be with the terms of the contract considered in light of the circumstances existing when the contract was made.

. . . .

Conclusion
 Because the trial court and the appellate court did not feel that enforcement could be refused, no findings were made on the possible unconscionability of the contracts in these cases. Since the record is not sufficient for our deciding the issue as a matter of law, the cases must be remanded to the trial court for further proceedings.
 So ordered.

proximity of background and holding; provides overview

alignment of major headings

procedural facts separated

aligned headings; both arguments summarized

flush-left **alignment** of subheadings A & B; **repeated** underlining

second **alignment** indented for subheads and **repeated** numbers

helpful headings

Example 6A. Campus sexual harassment policy

SEXUAL HARASSMENT IS AGAINST THE LAW

introduction to
underlying law is
off-putting to
intended audience

no proximity of
headings

no contrast for
headings

Definitions

"Sexual harassment"—Title VII of the Civil Rights Act of 1964 (employees), Title IX of the Education Amendments of 1972 (students), and University law define sexual harassment as unwelcome sexual advances; requests for sexual favors and other verbal or physical conduct of a sexual nature when submission to such conduct is made a term or condition of one's academic or employment status or is used as a basis for academic or employment decision; or conduct that unreasonably interferes with one's academic pursuits or working conditions by creating a hostile environment.

"*Quid pro quo* harassment"—When a person with authority in the university uses submission to or rejection of unwelcome sexual conduct as the basis for making academic or employment decisions affecting a subordinate, that action is sexual harassment.

"Harasser"—Sexual harassment can occur between supervisors and subordinates, faculty or staff and students, students' peers or co-workers, contractors or visitors and students, or any co-mbination of these.

"Prohibited conduct"—This includes subtle or overt pressure for sexual activity, unnecessary and unwanted touching or brushing against another's body, stalking, sexually suggestive visual displays and/or obscene messages, deliberate assaults or molestations, demands for sexual favors, or promises of preferential treatment or gifts in exchange for sex.

"Unwelcome behavior"—Behavior will be considered unwelcome if the individual did not solicit or invite it and particularly if he or she indicates that the conduct is undesirable or offensive. Acquiescence or failure to complain does not mean that the conduct is welcome. However, if a student or employee actively participates in sexual banter or discussions without giving an indication that the discussion is offensive, it will not be considered unwelcome.

How to report sexual harassment

Report the incident to the dean of students or the equal opportunity officer. Employees, including students who are employed here, who experience sexual harassment in their workplace should report it to a supervisor or the equal opportunity officer. All complaints and related documents will be maintained in a confidential file, and every attempt will be made to ensure the privacy of the individual and the respondent, subject to the university's legal obligations to take necessary disciplinary steps. If it is determined that sexual harassment has occurred, the university will proceed with disciplinary action with or without agreement from the complainant.

Example 6B. Revised sexual harassment policy

SEXUAL HARASSMENT IS AGAINST THE LAW

leading questions
contrast through
bold headings

What is sexual harassment?	What conduct is prohibited?
Sexual harassment is	**The law prohibits**

repetition of bold
tag lines for lists

Sexual harassment is
- unwelcome sexual advances;
- requests for sexual favors and other verbal or physical conduct of a sexual nature when submission to that conduct is made a term or condition of one's academic or employment status or is used as a basis for academic or employment decision; or
- conduct that unreasonably interferes with one's academic pursuits or working conditions by creating a hostile environment.

The law prohibits
- subtle or overt pressure for sexual activity,
- unnecessary and unwanted touching or brushing against another's body,
- stalking, sexually suggestive visual displays and/or obscene messages,
- deliberate assaults or molestations,
- demands for sexual favors, or
- promises of preferential treatment or gifts in exchange for sex.

Example: You are a work-study student and your boss often puts her arm around you or invites you home after work. You refuse those invitations and dread going to work.

proximity of
items in list

alignment of
bullet dots

specific action
example

Who might be a "harasser"?

How will someone determine "unwelcome" behavior?

question format
repeated, aligned

Sexual harassment can occur between supervisors and subordinates, faculty or staff and students, students, peers or co-workers, contractors or visitors and students, or any combination of these.

When **a person with authority** in the university uses submission to or rejection of unwelcome sexual conduct as the basis for making academic or employment decisions affecting a subordinate, that action is *quid pro quo* harassment.

Behavior will be considered unwelcome if the individual **did not invite** it and particularly if he or she indicates that the conduct is undesirable or offensive. Failure to complain does not mean that the conduct is welcome.

However, if a student or employee actively participates in sexual banter without indicating that the discussion is offensive, it will not be considered unwelcome.

two main points
highlighted with
bold face

Title VII of the Civil Rights Act of 1964 (employees), Title IX of the Education Amendments of 1972 (students), and University law.

Example: You are in an office where many of your male co-workers tell jokes about women and sex. You always break away from the group and change the subject.

repeated action
example

heavy line
detaches source
from information

97

Example 7A. Traditional class-action public notice

NOTICE OF PROPOSED SETTLEMENT

TO: All persons who purchased an "over the range" microwave oven manufactured by Whirlpool Corporation and sold under the Whirlpool, Kenmore, or KitchenAid brand name during the period from January 1, 1998, through September 30, 2001, with a serial number beginning with the letters "XC," and who have not suffered any personal injury or property damage as a result of a fire caused by such a microwave oven.

THIS LEGAL NOTICE MAY AFFECT YOUR RIGHTS. PLEASE READ IT CAREFULLY.

Si usted desea obtener una copia de este documento legal en Español, favor de actuar inmediatamente y visite la página web www.MHCSettlement.com o escribe al Administrador de Reclamos: Whirlpool MHC Settlement Administrator, P.O. Box 6175, Novato, CA 94948-6175. Your rights may be affected by a class action lawsuit pending in this Court, *Sonja Tuck and Carolyn Bogard v. Whirlpool Corp. and Sears, Roebuck and Co.*, Cause No. 49C01-0111-CP-002701. On February 7, 2003, this Court certified the following Settlement Class for settlement purposes only: All persons in the United States (including the District of Columbia) and its principal territories (Guam, the Commonwealth of Puerto Rico, and the Virgin Islands) who purchased a microwave-oven/hood combination manufactured by Whirlpool Corporation and sold under the Whirlpool, Kenmore, or KitchenAid brand name during the period from January 1, 1998, through September 30, 2001, with a serial number beginning with the letters "XC" ("MHC"). Excluded from the class are all persons who suffered personal injury or property damage as a result of a fire caused by such an MHC. If you own a microwave oven described above, you may be a member of the Settlement Class. **If your microwave oven has already been repaired pursuant to the recall** Whirlpool has been conducting since October 2001 (the "MHC Recall"), do not be concerned that the repair is inadequate or that your microwave is unsafe. The recall repair has been thoroughly considered and approved by the U.S. Consumer Product Safety Commission, and there is no claim in this lawsuit that the repair is inadequate in any way. **If, however, your microwave has not been repaired in the recall, you should immediately stop using it and call Whirlpool at 1-800-785-8897** to register for a free in-home repair and free extended warranty. The Court has named Sonja Tuck and Carolyn Bogard ("Plaintiffs") as representatives of the Settlement Class and their attorneys, Irwin B. Levin and Richard E. Shevitz as Class Counsel. Plaintiffs allege that Whirlpool and Sears breached express and implied warranties when they sold microwave-oven/hood combinations ("MHCs") that Whirlpool subsequently recalled because, if they have not been repaired pursuant to the recall, the MHCs present a fire risk of a type not found in other microwave ovens. Whirlpool and Sears deny Plaintiffs' allegations and assert defenses to Plaintiffs' claims. The Court has not ruled on the merits of the claims or defenses. Instead, the parties have entered into a Settlement Agreement. The Court has preliminarily approved the settlement provided for in the Settlement Agreement, but the settlement will not take effect unless it is finally approved by the Court after a public Final Approval Hearing. The Court will hold the Final Approval Hearing on July 7, 2003, at 9:00 a.m., in the Circuit Court for Marion County, Indiana, at 200 East Washington Street, Indianapolis, Indiana 46204. In the Settlement Agreement, Whirlpool has agreed to establish a Settlement Fund from which valid claims of Settlement Class members, and Class Counsel's attorneys' fees and expenses, will be paid. Whirlpool has agreed that it will pay from the Settlement Fund the sum of $7.50, or, in certain circumstances, a pro rata share of the Settlement Fund, to each Settlement Class member who meets the following criteria: (a) You have not requested and will not request to be excluded from the Settlement Class; (b) you owned an MHC unit on October 16, 2001; (c) as of October 16, 2001, the MHC was installed in a residence of which you were the owner or lessee; (d) after you learned of the MHC Recall, you stopped using your MHC until it could be repaired; (e) you have had your MHC repaired pursuant to the MHC Recall; (f) you have not already received from Whirlpool or Sears, in connection with the MHC Recall, a free countertop microwave oven, reimbursement for the purchase of a countertop microwave oven, a replacement MHC, a refund of the purchase price you paid for your original MHC, a gift certificate, or a cash payment; and (g) you timely sign under penalty of perjury and submit to the Settlement Administrator a Claim Form stating and affirming all of the information required above and the model and serial numbers of your MHC. Members of the Settlement Class who do not satisfy all these criteria will not share in the proceeds of the settlement. The Settlement Fund will be in the total amount of $7,974,570.00. Payments from it will be made, however, only upon (1) timely submission of a valid Claim Form to the Settlement Administrator, (2) approval of the claim by the Settlement Administrator, and (3) final judicial approval of the Settlement Agreement. If it approves the settlement, the Court will determine the amount of attorneys' fees and expenses to be paid from the Settlement Fund to Class Counsel for their efforts on behalf of the Settlement Class. Class Counsel has agreed not to petition the Court for an award of attorneys' fees and expenses exceeding 30 percent of the Settlement Fund. The payment to Class Counsel may reduce the funds available to the Settlement Class. If the settlement receives final judicial approval, it will result in a release, by Plaintiffs and all members of the Settlement Class who do not timely request exclusion from the settlement, of claims as specified in the Settlement Agreement, which released claims do not include claims for personal injury or property damage. If you believe you are a member of the Settlement Class, you have a choice whether to remain a member of the Settlement Class. You may (i) remain a member of the Settlement Class and submit a Claim Form to the Settlement Administrator; (ii) exclude yourself from the Settlement Class; (iii) object to the proposed settlement; (iv) retain your own attorney to appear on your behalf in this lawsuit; or (v) appear on your own behalf in this lawsuit. Your choice will have consequences that you should understand before making your decision. If you fail to submit the Claim Form in the manner and time specified in the Court's full Settlement Notice, you will waive any right to obtain payment from the Settlement Fund. To obtain the Court's full Settlement Notice explaining your rights and how to exercise each of the above options, a copy of the Claim Form, or more information regarding the proposed settlement, you should immediately contact the Settlement Administrator by visiting www.MHCSettlement.com, sending a request by e-mail to claimformrequest@MHCSettlement.com, calling the toll-free telephone number 1-888-429-6356, or mailing a self-addressed envelope to Whirlpool MHC Settlement Administrator, P.O. Box 6175, Novato, CA 94948-6175. The preceding description does not supersede the terms of the Settlement Agreement and related documents. To see the complete Court file, you may visit the Marion County Circuit Court, 200 East Washington Street, Indianapolis, Indiana, during regular business hours. If you believe you may be a member of the Settlement Class and have not received a full Settlement Notice and Claim Form by mail, please contact the Settlement Administrator, by e-mail, telephone, or mail, and provide your current address to which the Settlement Administrator can mail a full Settlement Notice and Claim Form.

If you have questions, contact:

WWW.MHCSETTLEMENT.COM OR 1-888-429-6356

Do not contact the Court, Whirlpool, or Sears regarding the settlement.

Dated: <u>February 7, 2003</u>

<u>/s/ Theodore M. Sosin</u>
Judge, Marion County Circuit Court

Example 7B. Revised class-action notice

LEGAL NOTICE

If you are a woman, and you are or were employed by XYZ, this class action notice may affect your rights.

You may be affected by a class action lawsuit about whether XYZ, Inc. discriminated against women on the basis of gender and age.

The case is in the United States District Court for the District of State, called *Johnson v. XYZ, Inc.,* No. CV-00-1234. The Court decided this lawsuit should be a class action on behalf of a "Class," or group of people, that could include you. This summarizes your rights and options. More information is in a detailed notice available at the website below. If you're included, you have to decide whether to stay in the Class and be bound by the results, or exclude yourself and keep the right to pursue your own lawsuit. **There is no money available to now and no guarantee that there will be.**

ARE YOU AFFECTED?

Women employed by XYZ, Inc., at any time between October 27, 1981 and July 15, 2000, are Class Members. This includes women currently employed, as long as they were hired before July 15, 2000, as well as those previously employed during the October 27, 1981 to July 15, 2000 Class period. XZY officers and directors, as well as **those who worked at XYZ through a "temp" agency or staffing service are NOT included**.

WHAT IS THIS CASE ABOUT?

The lawsuit claims that XYZ discriminated against women, by making it harder to get promoted. The suit claims women were treated unequally and got less pay than men in similar jobs. It also says that XYZ terminated older women more often, and didn't promote them as easily. The lawsuit seeks policies to ensure an equal workplace for women of any age, including a better arbitration and greivance procedure, as well as money or benefits for the Class.

XYZ denies it did anything wrong and says that it has a fair workplace that gives women the same oppurtunities as men. **The Court has not decided whether the Plaintiffs or Defendants are right.** The Plaintiffs will have to prove their claims at a trial set to begin on Month 00, 0000.

Are you affected?

- **Women now employed by XYZ, who were hired before July 15, 2000.**

- **Women previously employed by XYZ any time between October 27, 1981 and July 15, 2000.**

WHO REPRESENTS YOU?

The Court asked Lawfirm One, LLP of City, ST and Lawfirm Two, P.C. of City, ST, to represent you as "Class Counsel." You don't have to pay Class Counsel, or pay any money to participate. Instead, if they get money or benefits for the Class, they may ask the Court for attorneys' fees and costs, which would be paid by XYZ, or out of any money recovered, before giving the rest to the Class. You may hire your own lawyer to appear in Court for you, and if you do, you you have to pay that lawyer. Mary Johnson is a Class Member like you, and the Court accepted her as the "Class Representative."

WHAT ARE YOUR OPTIONS?

You have a choice of whether to stay in the Class or not, and you must decide this now. If you stay in the Class, you will be legally bound by all orders and judgments of the Court, and you won't be able to sue, or continue to sue, XYZ—as part of any other lawsuit—for gender and/or age discrimination that occurred during the Class period. If money or benefits are obtained in this case, you will be notified about how to get a share, or how to exclude yourself from any settlement. **To stay in the Class, you do not have to do anything now.**

If you don't want any money or benefits from this lawsuit, but you want to keep rights to sue XYZ for these claims, now or in the future, you must exclude yourself from the Class. To exclude yourself, send a letter to the address below, postmarked by **Month 00, 0000**, that says you want to be excluded from *Johnson v. XYZ, Inc.,* and includes your name, address, and telephone number. You can also get an exclusion request form at the website.

HOW CAN I GET MORE INFORMATION?

If you have questions, write to: XYZ Class Action, P.O. Box 000, City, ST 00000-0000. Visit the website below for a detailed notice, exclusion form, and other documents about this case and your rights.

www.xyzclassaction.com

Example 8A. Publication paragraphs with blocks of text

solid blocks of
information

all-cap titles hard
to read

no contrast, no
hierarchy of
information

The State Bar is required to offer CONTINUING LEGAL EDUCATION seminars throughout the state, throughout the year. As part of that mandate, CONTINUING LEGAL EDUCATION courses are offered this month in Alexandria, Annandale, Burke, Centreville, Fairfax, Lorton, Oakton, Reston, Vienna, and Falls Church. The CONTINUING EDUCATION classes will cover topics as diverse as ESTATE PLANNING, FEDERAL CRIMINAL LITIGATION, SECURITIES REGULATIONS, PROFESSIONAL SPORTS AND THE LAW, and FEDERAL AND STATE INDIAN LAW. Each course will be offered for three hours, and repeated twice during the month at each site.

Registration for these courses can be by mail, fax, or e-mail. Registrants must include their bar card number, their date of birth, application fee, and telephone number. Registrants are informed by this notice that they can receive no refund, but the registration fee can be applied to future CONTINUING LEGAL EDUCATION courses. The State Bar must receive the registration form and money five days before the course is presented. An acknowledgement will be sent to the registrant's address, plus a copy will be kept at the entrance to the seminar. Seminars will be conducted by state-certified attorneys with expertise in the field.

Example 8B. Revised paragraphs with variety and side bar

CONTINUING LEGAL EDUCATION

contrast size and type face

The State Bar offers Continuing Legal Education seminars throughout the state, throughout the year. Continuing Legal Education courses are offered this month in

- Alexandria
- Annandale
- Burke
- Centreville
- Fairfax
- Lorton
- Oakton
- Reston
- Vienna
- Falls Church

proximity of items

TOPICS

Estate Planning
Federal Criminal Litigation
Securities Regulations
Professional Sports and the Law
Federal and State Indian Law

alignment

Each course will be offered for three hours and repeated twice during the month at each site. Seminars will be conducted by state-certified attorneys with expertise in the field.

Registration
Registration for these courses can be by mail, fax, or e-mail.

repetition of type face and **alignment**

Registrants must include their
    bar card number,
    date of birth,
    application fee, and
    telephone number.

proximity and **alignment**

Although you can receive no refund, your registration fee can be applied to future CONTINUING LEGAL EDUCATION courses.

repetition, contrasting type face

The registration form and money must be received five days before the course is presented.

contrast with bold

An acknowledgement will be sent to the registrant's address, plus a copy will be kept at the entrance to the seminar.

CONCLUDING EXERCISE

Work with the information below and create a **cover letter** for a post-graduate job at the medium-sized law firm of Smith & Smith, which has an opening in family law and an opening in litigation. S & S attorney/personnel director Ron Dublanski placed an advertisement in *Illinois Lawyer* announcing two, possibly three, openings for lawyer applicants with none-to-three years experience. What skills would Jennifer highlight, given her goals? What organizational scheme would she use? See possible answers, page 117.

Jennifer Long
1818 S. Congress Ave.
Chicago, Illinois 60633
773-834-4409
jlong@aol.com

J.D. University of Chicago expected May 2005, 3.39 g.p.a.
Special courses: Trial Advocacy, Children's Rights Clinic
Staff member: Children and the Law Journal, Women and Legal Times
    Journal
Undergraduate: M.A., Chicago-Kent 2001, Social Work
                B.A., Chicago- Kent 1995, Social Work
Work: City of Chicago Child Protection Office (investigator),
        1995-1998
        District Attorney's Office, Chicago, paralegal, 2001-2002
Skills: clear prose, interviewing, keeping clear records, data spread
        sheets, oral argument
Hobbies: Jennifer Lopez memorabilia, hiking
Ref: Prof. Anne Smith, trial advocacy, University of Chicago
    Michael Moore, District Attorney's Office, Chicago
Career goals: I want to practice law in a small family-law firm or with
            an agency that specializes in family law. After a few years,
            I want to do both trial work and appellate work.

ANSWERS TO "TRY THESE" AND CONCLUDING EXERCISES

CHAPTER 1: ORGANIZATION

Try These Headings from pages 7-9

1. No, they do not follow the setup.

    a. The court will find Grimes' procedural errors to be negligence.

    b. An investigation of the client contract will reveal whether Grimes breached the contract.

c. The court will reject any DTPA claims because Grimes did not knowingly misfile or misrepresent his client.

2. Headings should follow the setup.

a. The Sixth Amendment requires effective assistance.

b. Case law requires thorough research.

c. Rule of Appellate Procedure 38.1 provides guidelines for brief form.

3. The paragraph is incomplete without its thesis.

C. The Oregon Supreme Court does not recognize an exception for lawyer dishonesty.

The Oregon Supreme Court, in the recent *In re Gatti*, 8 P.3d 966 (Or. 2000), sanctioned a lawyer who misrepresented his identity while attempting to investigate a claim of insurance fraud. Thus, the Oregon court refused to recognize "an exception for any lawyer to engage in dishonesty." Id. at 976. Not all states adopt as strict an approach. New York, for example, has long recognized prosecutorial exceptions to the dishonesty rule.

Try This Micro Organization from pages 16-17

Jones & Jones (J & J) hired 35 summer associates for its Dallas office, including second-year law student Annette Noel. Despite her first-year Legal Research and Writing course, she knew little about researching; indeed, she knew only that federal and state laws were both dependent and independent.

On Friday afternoon, July 5, Gerald Gerardi asked Ms Noel to research and write a memo on Texas regulations for food safety and pesticides by Monday at 9 a.m. Because Ms Noel's family imported pottery and she had a business degree, she understood the general topic but not what Mr. Gerardi specifically needed. Nevertheless, over the weekend Ms Noel researched and wrote a 40-page memorandum without the aid of a law librarian. On Monday, Gerardi used her memo to file his brief for his biggest client, Lima, Inc.

On July 12, Ms Noel left for her second summer internship in New York City.

Concluding Exercises from pages 17-19

1. **Thesis and road maps.** Rule and facts present no thesis and no setup.

> Powe should probably not be sanctioned for a Rule 11 violation. Rule 11 of the Federal Rules of Civil Procedure requires attorneys to certify that any pleading or written motion is filed not to harass or to delay, and to certify that the claims and contentions are not frivolous. In the instant case, Powe believed that his motion on behalf of the teacher was backed by strong evidence that she had been discriminated against by her administration. He had no knowledge of a Fourth Circuit requirement that a client must go through collective bargaining as a member of a school district. Thus he counseled her not to ask for collective bargaining before the filing. **Because the facts show that Powe did not file to harass, delay, or present frivolous motions, he should not be sanctioned.**

   a. Rule 11 is intended to prevent frivolous filings.

   b. Powe had evidence of discrimination.

   c. A Fourth Circuit requirement for collective bargaining does not present an issue of frivolous filings.

2. **Road map paragraphs and headings.** The headings are **not** anticipated and thus not effective. Replace them with something like this:

a. Federal courts generally accept attorney evidence of good faith.

b. Federal courts are split on requiring collective bargaining.

3. Topic sentences and transitions

Attorneys have a duty of reasonable care to serve their clients. For example, in 1989 the Texas Supreme Court found, in <u>Walder v. Texas</u>, 85 S.W.3d 824, 829 (2002), that a counsel must serve a client to the best of his or her ability. In **Walder,** counsel did not identify the appropriate standard for appellate review of a revocation order. **More recently,** in 2002, the same court held that counsel had a duty to act as a reasonably prudent professional. <u>Cosgrove v. Grimes</u>, 774 S.W.2d 662 (1989). **There,** counsel did not recognize the statute of limitations in a car accident that occurred in another state. **Gerardi's issue** is whether an attorney's overlooking a major development in case law violates the standard of reasonable care.

4. Transitions

Pamela Hunter **filed a class-action suit** on behalf of a group of North Carolina bakery workers. **These workers** believed that their **company-owned** bakery had violated Title V11 of the Civil Rights Act of 1964 when the **owners** closed **this bakery** but not others. **The owners** had publicly stated that **this particular bakery** would remain open throughout the year.

Ms Hunter **alleged** that the bakery had a pattern and practice of racial discrimination. Compared to the predominately white workers at **other company-owned bakeries**, the predominately African-American workers in this bakery were more skilled but paid less. The bakery denied the **allegations** and **furthermore** insisted that any Title V11 claims had to be arbitrated under a collective bargaining agreement (**CBA**).

The bakery **then** argued that Hunter knew, or should have known, of the **CBA** and asked the court to impose a Rule 11 sanction on Ms Hunter for filing a lawsuit before arbitration. The

North Carolina court sanctioned her and suspended her legal practice for five years **although** five other circuits have held that Title VII claims do not have to be first arbitrated under CBA.

CHAPTER 2: SENTENCES

Try These Long Sentences from page 26

1. The determination of proximate cause is usually a question of fact. This is true in legal malpractice cases as well. **However, determining** causation in those cases requires determining whether the appeal in the underlying action would have been successful but for the attorney's negligence.

2. Lawyers who are not in the same firm may divide fees only **if:** the division is in proportion to the services provided or the client agrees; **the** lawyers assume joint responsibility for representation; **the** client is informed of the division, its terms, and the lawyers' participation and does not object; **and** the total fee is reasonable.

3. A lawyer cannot induce a client to make a substantial **gift (e.g.,** money, property, stock, or future money, property, stock, **etc.)** to the lawyer or the lawyer's parent, sibling, child, or spouse, except where the client is related to the attorney. **The lawyer may accept** a gift from the lawyer's client, **however**, subject to general standards of fairness and absence of undue influence.

Try These Front-Loaded Sentences from page 28

1.1 The words "fraudulent act" were deleted from the original 8.4(b), and language tracking Disciplinary Rule 1-102(A)(4) of the 1969 Code was inserted instead, **pursuant** to a proposal from the Iowa Bar Association at the 1983 Midyear Meeting of the ABA House of Delegates.

1.2 The Iowa Bar Association at the 1983 Midyear Meeting of the ABA House of Delegates proposed a change in language; the words "fraudulent act" were deleted from the original 8.4(b), and language tracking Disciplinary Rule 1-102(A)(4) of the 1969 Code was inserted.

2.1 The mere presence of an anomaly is not necessarily poor public policy **although** it is offensive to notions of aesthetic value and the sense that the Model Rules represent a coherent code.

2.2 The mere presence of an anomaly is not necessarily poor public policy. The anomaly may nevertheless be offensive to notions of aesthetic value and the sense that the Model Rules represent a coherent code.

Try These Awkward Citation Placements from page 30

1. **The four standards** of "negligent misrepresentation" are set forth in <u>Atkins v. Kirkpatrick</u>, 832 S.W.2d 547 (Tenn. Ct. App. 1991).

2. **Rule 11** of the Federal Rules of Civil Procedure **prohibits** attorneys from arguing a false claim or frivolously pursuing a material fact. One **sanctioned lawyer** believes that the Fourth Circuit court expanded the reach of Rule 11 when it held an attorney guilty for advocating against the precedent of the Fourth Circuit. <u>Hunter v. Earthgrains Co. Bakery</u>, 281 F.3d 144 (4th Cir. 2002).

3. **Section 1399** allows the employer to seek review of the schedule of payments. 29 U.S.C. § 1399(b)(2)(A)(i). However, this dispute also falls under **Section** 1401, the arbitration provision.

Try These Treacherous Placement from page 33

1. Robin Mayhem tried "at least 10 times" to leave Jamail Fenwick, father of her two baby boys. She said **Fenwick would beat** her regularly.

2. The rule, with all its attendant enforcement costs, results in **only** a marginal reduction instances of unethical behavior.

3a. After receiving the client's money, you must, **within two weeks of receipt,** deposit the check and have it listed as a separate account.

3b. After receiving the client's money, you must deposit the check **within two weeks of receipt.** You must also list it as a separate account.

Try These Faulty Parallelism from page 36

1. The doctrine of unconstitutional vagueness **(1) provides** for adequate notice of a rule and **(2) is** a safeguard against governmental abuse.

2. The plaintiff must show:

   a. a reasonable probability that the parties would enter into a contractual relationship;

   b. the defendant acted maliciously by intentionally preventing the relationship from occurring with the purpose of harming the plaintiff;

   c. the defendant was not privileged or justified; and

   d. actual harm or damage occurred as a result of the interference.

3. A lawyer may not engage in dishonesty, fraud, deceit, **or** misrepresentation; **nor** may a lawyer give false statements.

Try These Passive Voice from page 39

1. Researching **attorneys may find** the modern origins of the dishonesty rule in the 1908 American Bar Association (ABA) Canons of Professional Ethics.

2. The **committee held,** for example, that a lawyer violates the dishonesty rule if he assists a litigant who purports to appear *pro se,* but the litigant fails to notify the court that he is receiving the advice of counsel.

3. A **court would not strike** the law as unconstitutionally vague if the law were capable of being made reasonably clear through judicial interpretation.

Concluding Sentence Exercises from pages 43-45

1. [front-loaded] It is a lawyer's duty to safeguard confidential client information **if** there is a reasonable prospect that disclosing or using it will adversely affect a material interest of the client or if the client has instructed the lawyer not to use or disclose the information.

2. [lengthy quotations] Commentators have recognized that determination of causation in an appellate legal malpractice case is a question of law. Initially, the **court requires** the plaintiff to prove **that "but for** the attorney's negligence, the plaintiff should have prevailed upon the motion or appeal." 2 R. Mallen & J. Smith, *Legal Malpractice* §§ 24.39, at 536. (3d ed. 1989) **A trial judge must make the decision** as an issue of law, based on the transcript and record. **The decision is subject** to the same rules of review as should have been applied by the appellate court to the motion or appeal. Id.

3. [passive, truncated] A **member** of a law firm **must deposit** all funds received or held for the benefit of clients, including advances and expenses, into an identifiable bank account labeled "Trust Account" or words of similar import.

4. [long sentence] An **attorney** or unrepresented party, by presenting a pleading, motion, or other paper to the court, **is certifying** that he/she has a proper purpose. **The attorney certifies** that the filing is not being presented for any improper purpose. **The attorney is also certifying** that other legal contentions in the document are warranted by existing law and that other allegations and factual contentions have evidentiary support or are likely to have evidentiary support after a reasonable opportunity for further investigation or discovery. **Finally, the attorney certifies** that the denials of factual contentions are warranted on the evidence, or are reasonably based on a lack of information or belief.

5. [faulty parallelism] An **attorney cannot deposit** funds belonging to a member of a law firm into a client's Trust account unless they are funds to pay reasonable bank charges. **If** the client and firm member have collectively added the money to the account, then the law firm member must withdraw his/her amount as soon as possible.

6. [treacherous placement] You may not solicit a client from your previous law firm without that firm's **written** contract provision or **written** permission.

7. [awkward citation placement] That a lawyer engages in conduct that may be contrary to the Rules of Professional Conduct does not automatically give rise to a civil cause of action. *Noble v. Sears, Roebuck & Co,* 33 Cal. App. 3d 654 (1973). However, the disciplinary rules are not intended to supercede existing law relating to lawyers in non-disciplinary contexts. *Klemm v. Superior Court,* 75 Cal. App. 3d 893 (1977).

CHAPTER 3: WORDS

Try These Jargon from page 50

1. Attorney Don Miller refutes this charge and contends that he has been unfairly brought into this suit as a party.

2.1 She alleges violation of certain state law claims: fraud, breach of contract, and misrepresentation.

2.2 She alleges violation of certain state law claims, **specifically** fraud, breach of contract, and misrepresentation.

Try These Wordiness from page 54

1. to evaluate

2. said

3. The attorney was morally, but not legally, obligated.

Try These Pronoun Antecedents from page 56

1. The question is whether Smith informed others of the defect in the computer board design and **if this lack of information** caused the loss of benefits Dell expected from these companies.

2. If there are cases on point with similar fact situations and you are discussing an issue that calls for argument, **these similar facts** will give more weight to your argument.

3. A lawyer is subject to discipline if he makes a materially false statement in, or fails to disclose a material fact in connection with, application to the bar. Law school career service offices attempt to publicize **those possible mistakes.**

Try These Noun Strings from pages 57-58

1. certified, return-receipt postcard

2. funded welfare-insurance programs *or* funded-welfare insurance programs

3. the bank's credit-review service

Try These Nominalizations from page 59

1. After thoroughly **investigating** your deposition files, we suggest new coding. (*or* we suggest that you add a new code)

2. Thank you for allowing our firm **to present** international issues **related to** your business.

Try These Treacherous Words from page 65

1. **Because** the clerk had stood to attention, the court audience did also.

2. Attorney Fred Fudd recommended that Mrs. Baker hire someone to monitor her work and **ensure** that the premiums were properly dispersed.

3. The therapist posited various possible causes for the child's anxiety, **e.g.,** travel between two households, parental inability to communicate, participating in contrasting religious activities, etc.

Try These Gendered Words from page 68

1. Dear J.W. Smith [*or* check the Internet for bibliographic information, *or* call the person's assistant]

2. Use plural: . . . **artists** need insurance when **they** . . .

3. If time and logic permit, exchange the "he" with "she." If the entire document is on its way out the door, attach a note asking if your client would prefer that you ignore tradition and exchange the pronouns in future work you'll do for her.

Concluding Word Exercises from pages 68-69

1. The associate took many **late-night** excursions into the break room.

2. When the associate saw the secretary in the office after 10 p.m., she was worried that the **secretary** took her job too seriously.

3. **Although** she approached her job seriously, the firm's view was that **excessive** time would be deleted **immediately**.

4. A **supervisor determined** that extra time throughout her last time sheet was inappropriate.

5. The senior partner asked her **to state** why [*or* **to explain why**] she **objected** to the edit of her time sheets.

6. composed of

7. discreet

8. laid

9. infer

10. its

CHAPTER 4: PUNCTUATION

Concluding Punctuation Exercises from pages 80-81

1. **[comma needed after introductory phrase]** If confidence sinks too **low,** members of the public will cease looking to the legal system for resolution to problems.

2. **[semicolons needed for lists in which elements of list require commas]** A court must weigh the dangers of vagueness and discriminatory enforcement against the need to protect the integrity of the judicial **system;** the goal of protecting the interests of the client, which is admittedly **paternalistic;** and the need to encour-

age honesty among lawyers, which maintains the integrity of the profession.

3. **[comma needed after "counsel" because there are two independent clauses]** Some opinions have held that Rule 8.4(c) requires a lawyer to bring possible mistakes to the attention of opposing **counsel,** and others have held that a violation may occur through the acts or omissions of a third party.

4. **[period—or semicolon—needed or sentence is run-on]** It seeks first to avoid the need to abandon Rule 8.4(c) by proposing a framework for the analysis of future cases arising under the **rule. Second,** it attempts to focus attention to the dangers inherent in broad grants of judicial discretion.

5. **[colon, not a dash, before lists]** A court must weigh the dangers of vagueness and discriminatory enforcement against the **following:** the need to protect the integrity of the judicial system, the goal of protecting the interests of clients, and the need to encourage honesty among lawyers.

6. **[short quotations not indented]** When examining a statute, a court must ask whether the statute **either** "fails to give a person of ordinary intelligence fair notice that his contemplated conduct is forbidden by the statute, or is so indefinite that it encourages arbitrary and erratic arrests and **convictions."**

7. **[comma needed for nonessential information]** The rule creates an incentive on the part of a lawyer to avoid overly aggressive **conduct, which** might be construed as a violation. (If essential information, change to **that** and drop comma: The rule creates an incentive on the part of a lawyer to avoid overly aggressive conduct **that** might be construed as a violation.)

8. **[period placed inside quotation marks]** Canon 22 of the 1908 Canons imposed upon lawyers a general duty of "candor and **fairness."**

9. **[dash, colon, or comma sets off explanatory information]** Where an act of dishonesty has not injured a client or someone to whom the lawyer owes a fiduciary duty, then at least one goal of discipline is not **compromised—the** goal of protecting clients.

10. **[semicolon creates dependent clause (fragment); use either a dash or comma]** Given the problems with attorneys' ethics, some might argue that all law school courses should include discussions of ethical **issues—**specific issues with concrete examples. [*or* **issues,** specific issues with concrete examples.]

CHAPTER 5: FORMAT

Concluding Exercise from page 102

1818 S. Congress Avenue
Chicago, Illinois 60633
773-834-4409
jlong@aol.com

Smith & Smith
1717 Centerpoint
Chicago, Ill 60611

Re: Attorney Employment

identify job
opening

Dear Mr. Dublanski,

I saw your advertisement in *Illinois Lawyer* and am applying for a position as a family law attorney. My skills and my goals make me a good match for this job.

express
specific
interest

I am graduating from the University of Chicago Law School with a special concentration in family law and litigation. I took both the Children's Rights Clinic and Trial Advocacy, and spent most of my free time helping the clinic with family-law issues.

legal
education
background
that matches
opening

My work experience also parallels the Smith & Smith opening: I was an investigator for three years with the City of Chicago Child Protection Office. Just before law school, I worked for a year as a paralegal in the Chicago's District Attorney's Office, where I handled cases and issues in family law on a daily basis. My B.A. and M.A. in Social Work from Chicago-Kent gave me the theoretical framework for both jobs, and now my legal education has developed my understanding of the law behind the cases and situations I encountered.

work
experience
that matches
opening

educational
background

I am interested in both family law and litigation and plan to practice in the Chicago area. I would very much appreciate an opportunity to discuss your current openings.

link to city

professional
tone

Sincerely,

Jennifer Long

leaves
details to
resume

enclosure: resume

INDEX